P R A C T I C A L   G A R D E N I N G

HOUSEPLANTS

PRACTICAL GARDENING

HOUSEPLANTS

DAVID SQUIRE &
MARGARET CROWTHER

CHANCELLOR
PRESS

First published in Great Britain in 1995 by
C H A N C E L L O R   P R E S S
an imprint of Reed Consumer Books Limited
Michelin House, 81 Fulham Road, London SW3 6RB
and Auckland, Melbourne, Singapore and Toronto

ISBN 1-85152-841-5

A CIP catalogue record for this book
is available from the British Library

Designed and produced by
THE BRIDGEWATER BOOK COMPANY
Art Director and Designer Terry Jeavons
Managing Editor Anna Clarkson
Series Editor Penny David
Illustrator Vana Haggerty
Studio photography Guy Ryecart *assisted by Jim Clowes*
Location photography Steve Wooster *assisted by Carolyn Clegg*
Typesetting and page make up Mark Woodhams

Produced by Mandarin Offset
Printed and bound in Hong Kong

A C K N O W L E D G E M E N T S
*The authors would like to thank Anna Clarkson, Managing Editor,
for her dedication to the production of this book.*

The Bridgewater Book Company would like to thank the following for their cooperation:
Hollygate Cactus Garden, Ashington (Mr and Mrs S. Chatwin); Kennedys Garden Centre, Hailsham (John Phillips);
Stone Cross Nursery, Pevensey (Garth and Julie Winwood, Alick Janaway); Wyevale Garden Centre, Lewes (Martin Rayment); Hugh and Judy Johnson (Saling Hall);
Sue Farrell; David & Yvonne Gregory; Jonathan & Madeleine Hilton; Maxine & Chris Pascal; Mr & Mrs Relph; The Palm Centre, Surrey;
Terry Hewitt & The Hollygate Cactus Nursery, West Sussex; Lorraine & Peter Bridgewater.
Special thanks to Alex Martin & Des Whitwell of Chessington Nurseries.

CONTENTS

INTRODUCTION

A house, or a flat, is not a home without houseplants. Whether it be a welcome stranger in the form of a pot plant or 'gift' plant that changes with the seasons or an old friend in the form of a long-lived plant in a permanent position, plants bring the place to life. It may or may not be the case that plants respond to being talked to, but they certainly respond to good care. This means being aware of the sort of conditions in which similar plants grow in the wild, and meeting houseplants' needs in respect of compost type, the level of light, the degree of moisture, humidity and temperature, winter and summer, the amount of fertilizer necessary at different times of year, and any other attention they need to reward you with strong growth, a good shape, healthy leaves and beautiful flowers. And whether or not plants respond to people except by flourishing when well cared for, people certainly respond to plants, and feel better for their presence in the home.

KITCHENS AND BATHROOMS

In kitchens, cupboard doors are opened and shut, windows and doors need to be opened, surfaces need to be kept free; heat levels can change dramatically when cooking is in progress, and cupboard tops can get all the rising heat making them inhospitable places for many plants. It is best to reserve the kitchen for inexpensive plants and plants that will not get in the way: easy-care green plants, perhaps hung on wall brackets, and undemanding flowering plants on windowsills.

Bathrooms too are first and foremost functional even though they can also be havens of privacy and comfort. They are often advocated as ideal areas for growing plants that love humidity, but not all bathrooms are humid all the time and their temperature here can fluctuate widely also. Again, it may be better to choose tolerant plants rather than exotic rainforest species.

A large handsome plant such as this Boston Fern (*Nephrolepis exaltata* 'Bostoniensis') is a perfect specimen plant, and the pedestal table allows the fronds to arch to their full length.

RIGHT As lovers of humidity ferns are often displayed in bathrooms. The unusual staghorn fern (*Platycerium bifurcatum*) has quite striking architectural qualities which make it blend well with plain white bathroom fittings and classic brass water taps.

MAIN ROOMS

Living rooms, dining rooms and bedrooms, in comparison, are places of peace and tranquillity, and likely to have more constant temperatures and fewer draughts. In living and dining rooms plants can be displayed in troughs or in floor-standing groups, in fireplaces, on windowsills and on tables. Large floor-standing specimens in big pots make a superb focal point.

Bedrooms are often cooler and this is useful for ferns, cyclamen, azaleas and other plants which need slightly lower temperatures. There are plenty of plants for cooler conditions, from impressive ferns to dainty primroses. Unheated spare bedrooms are often the best place in the house for plants that need a dormant period during the winter and for growing plants from seeds and cuttings.

HALLS, LANDINGS AND PASSAGES

Circulation spaces can be draughty or may have low light levels, and they are areas where people may be rushing about, and likely to knock over plants that are not carefully positioned. Here large specimens can stand in corners, trailing plants can hang in baskets and foliage plants, or pot plants on a hall table create a welcoming atmosphere.

The long-lived yucca (*Yucca elephantipes*) makes a permanent houseplant feature. Bold plants such as this need sturdy pots, both visually and to take their weight. This yucca produces leaves up to 90cm (3ft) long.

ABOVE RIGHT
A small and lightly perfumed plant such as Arabian violet (*Exacum affine*) is ideal for a pretty, feminine bedroom.

ABOVE
A conservatory provides the opportunity to create an indoor garden of ferns and greenery, with height and space for tall plants and vigorous climbing and trailing plants. Small plants can be grown around their base. By dampening the tiled floor, the air can be kept moist and cool.

LEFT Plants bring a dining area to life. Keeping them in separate pots means that larger plants, such as the Kaffir lily (*Clivia miniata*), can be removed from the table when more space is needed, while small plants can remain as table decoration.

RANGE OF HOUSEPLANTS

Houseplants come in all shapes and sizes, slow and fast growing, long and short lived, leafy or flowering. From a designer's point of view they can be roughly divided according to their appearance. There are rosette-forming and bushy plants, from small to large, suitable for table tops, windowsills and arranging in groups. Plants which climb or trail are candidates for hanging baskets, training on screens and up poles, standing on plinths, shelves and high windowsills, or simply, when young, for training up canes or round hoops as windowsill plants. Finally, there are specimen plants of various kinds, from enormous ferns for containers on stands and high display tables to air-rooting climbers for large mossy poles and weeping figs and other plants with tree-like shapes. From a botanist's point of view plants are divided into families and known partly for their place of origin, and in this book we have borrowed from both these approaches, dividing plants partly by type and partly by function, making distinctions which inevitably partly overlap.

The bromeliads (see pages 93–95) include many rosette-forming leathery-leaved plants such as the popular urn plant (*Aechmea fasciata*). It is watered by filling the urn with water.

Cacti (see pages 98–105) are distinctive plants from hot parts of the world with conspicuous spines and well-defined shapes, as in the column cactus (*Cereus peruvianus*).

Flowering pot plants (see pages 54–57) are the 'gift' plants, which, like cyclamen (*Cyclamen persicum*), do not necessarily survive more than one season as houseplants.

Most houseplants are grown either mainly for their flowers or mainly for their foliage, but within these two groups there is a wealth of choice: seasonal or almost all-year flowering, perfumed flowers, climbing and trailing plants, plants with bold foliage that reward with a burst of flowers, plants whose leaves are as colourful as flowers, plants for sun rooms and conservatories and plants for cool rooms. Certain plants have special status: palms, ferns and bromeliads, cacti and other succulents all have distinctive features of their own, and then there are plants grown for their

colourful berries or fruits, tropical insectivorous plants, and, of course, the wealth of flowering plants grown indoors from bulbs.

Although many plants are widely known by their common names, these can vary from country to country, even from person to person. So to be sure of identifying a plant correctly it is always safer to use its Latin or botanical name. Even botanical names may change from time to time, however, and when this has occurred, we have given both the old and the new names to avoid any confusion.

LEFT Large foliage plants such as variegated weeping fig (*Ficus benjamina* 'Golden King') gain from being arranged with other leafy plants – here the bird's nest fern (*Asplenium nidus*) and kalanchoe (*Kalanchoe blossfeldiana*), well-chosen objects heighten the effect.

Ferns (see pages 86–91) can be delicate, feathery and lacy, or, like the bird's nest fern (*Asplenium nidus*), boldly broad-leaved.

Daffodils (*Narcissus* species) are among the most popular of all the bulbous plants (see pages 58–65). The bulbs are planted in autumn to flower in late winter or early spring.

Dracaena deremensis is a superb foliage plant that is available in several variegated forms. Eventually it grows to 1.2m (4ft) or more and forms a fine specimen plant (see pages 66–7 and 76–7).

DISPLAYING PLANTS

There are endless ways of displaying plants. The simplest is, of course, to stand a single plant alone in its pot, in a place where it gets the right amount of light – usually on a windowsill – or to replant it in an attractive container or hide the utilitarian pot in a cache pot. But plants often look better, and grow better, in a group. They can be grouped with their pots on show or arranged with the pots hidden in a container such as a trough, or they may be planted together in a container to form a sort of indoor garden.

Certain plants dictate to some extent the way in which they should be displayed. Very large plants need large, floor-standing pots – they do not necessarily have to be displayed as single specimens. A group of plants with perhaps a palm as its main element, grading down through large and medium-sized foliage plants and ferns, and softened with trailing ivy, can be a stunning feature in a room with high ceilings, plain-painted walls and simple furniture. This sort of arrangement can be enhanced by a large mirror used to reflect the leaves or spotlighting to create highlights and shadows. Climbers and trailers must be allowed room and a hanging basket or a plant stand is perfect for trailers. Small climbers can be grown up canes or round hoops and vigorous climbers can be trained over wires or trellis to form room dividers, obscure an ugly view or adorn a conservatory wall. Moisture-loving, draught-fearing plants can be planted together in a glass terrarium, bottle garden or Wardian case to make a beautiful and interesting centrepiece.

A mass of crocuses planted closely together in a terracotta pot makes a burst of early spring colour. The sphagum moss provides the finishing touch.

CARE AND GROOMING

Well-groomed plants make for the best display. Choose a watering-can with a long spout to make watering easy and buy a mist spray so that you can regularly spray with tepid, lime free water the many plants that need humidity. Standing plants on pebbles in trays or bowls of water is an attractive way of providing additional humidity.

Cut off dead flowers with sharp scissors and secateurs. Check on the requirements for individual plants, and pinch out growing points to keep them bushy, or snip them into shape as necessary. Clean the leaves of foliage plants with a cloth wrung out in tepid water. Watch out for pests and diseases, and treat them promptly.

LEFT A specimen foliage plant (*Dracaena marginta*, the Madagascar dragon tree) makes an outstanding feature in any room when it is set against plain white walls and reflected by a large mirror.

LEFT All sorts of containers can be used to add character to a plant display. This ornate birdcage shows off a flaming Katy (*Kalanchoe blossfeldiana*) in a novel and attractive way, adding an extra dimension to a simple pot plant.

Plant stands were *de rigueur in* Victorian and Edwardian days and are now back in fashion. They are purpose-made for plants with arching growth. An elegant white ceramic pedestal and matching pot turn this humble spider plant (*Chlorophytum comosum*) into a worthy specimen and show off its trailing plantlets dramatically.

This beautiful terrarium provides an interesting and unusual container for a pretty display of *Pellaea rotundifolia, Adiantum capillus-veneris, Chamaedorea elegans, Hypoestes sanguinocenta* and *Selaginella.*

BUYING, POTS AND COMPOSTS

Choosing houseplants needs as much care as buying any other item for a home. The plant needs to fit in with its surroundings, as well as to create an attractive display. Additionally, it is essential to buy a healthy plant that will create a display over a long period. Buying a low-cost plant that dies within a few weeks often proves to be a mistake. Check plants and discard those with roots coming out of drainage holes, with wilting leaves, infested with pests and diseases, or where the compost and pot are covered with moss or slime. Also, do not buy plants displayed outdoors in hot sunshine or in draughts.

Getting plants home quickly and safely and acclimatizing them to indoor life is also important. Ensure that the garden centre or nursery wraps your plant; this prevents draughts blowing on them and reduces the chance of knocks damaging leaves and flowers. Do not place plants in car boots or trunks if the weather is extremely hot or cold. Instead, stand them upright in boxes inside the car. When the plants reach home, unpack them and position in a lightly-shaded, draught-free position in gentle warmth for about a week. Water the compost. If a few buds or leaves initially fall off, do not worry as the plant is probably just settling down. During this initial period, check that the plant is not contaminated with pests and diseases.

CLAY AND PLASTIC POTS
The sizes of pots range from 36mm (1½in) to 38cm (15in) wide (across their tops). Mostly, four sizes are used: 6cm (2½in), 7.5cm (3in), 13cm (5in) and 18cm (7in). Large, floor-standing plants may need a 25cm (10in) pot. There are complementary saucers in which pots can be stood.

Clay pots are traditional containers for plants. They create a firm base and harmonize with leaves and flowers. Their porous nature enables excess moisture to evaporate through the sides and toxic salts can escape in the same way. But, especially for plants that need a peat-type compost, plastic pots are sometimes preferred. As moisture does not evaporate through these pots it is important not to overwater.

If a plant is wilting, this can be caused by lack of moisture or by waterlogged compost. Pests such as root mealy bugs cause similar problems.

Plants in small pots can sometimes be rescued by repotting them immediately although if the roots are matted this can retard – or prevent – recovery.

When buying houseplants, reject those with moss or slime on the pot or surface of the compost. This reveals neglect and indicates that the plant's roots are severely congested; even if repotted immediately, it is doubtful if the plant would recover.

Never buy plants that are in full flower, as their display soon will be diminished. Preferably, buy flowering plants which have a few buds that show colour, and many more waiting to open. Also, do not buy flowering plants that are wilting.

Look for plants that are 'in balance' with the pot. Do not buy small plants that are growing in large pots (it is then difficult to keep the compost evenly moist) or large plants in small pots (the compost dries very rapidly).

ENVIRONMENTALLY FRIENDLY COMPOSTS

Peat-free composts are the most recent development in composts and they are becoming increasingly popular as they do not involve the continued destruction of the natural habitat of many plants and animals.

The main ingredient in these composts is generally coir, obtained from the husk of a coconut – a material much used in the past for making ropes and matting.

Gardeners are usually devotees of either peat- or loam-based composts, but it is worth experimenting with a coir-based type which in many ways has much the same qualities as peat, such as moisture retention and aeration. There are ready-to-use seed and potting composts based on coir and, after use, the compost can be re-used as a mulch around outdoor plants.

In the future, composts formed of materials such as straw, bark and wood fibre may also be available.

LOAM- AND PEAT-BASED COMPOSTS

These provide anchorage for plants and moisture, food and air for roots. Garden soil is unsuitable for houseplants as its quality is variable. It is also badly drained and may contain weed seeds, pests and diseases. Specially prepared composts are therefore needed; there are two types.

Loam-based composts are formed from partially sterilized loam (good topsoil), peat and sharp sand, plus fertilizers. These composts are:
* heavier than other types and give stability to large plants;
* unlikely to dry out as fast or so completely as the other types;
* richer in minor and trace plant foods than other types of compost;
* capable of growing most houseplants.

Peat-based composts are a more recent development than loam-based types. They are:
* more uniform in quality than loam-based composts;
* liable to dry out more rapidly than soil-based types and are difficult to remoisten;
* lighter to carry home by the bag than loam-based composts;
* poorer in nutrients than loam-based composts, so be prepared to feed plants at an earlier stage;
* easily stored even after the bag is opened – just fold over and tie the end;
* when stored in garden centres or nurseries, the peat often becomes compacted. Therefore, before using the compost, shake the bag thoroughly to loosen it.

There is only one hole in the base of a clay pot. This is covered by a crock (piece of broken clay pot) and loam-based compost is used when repotting a plant.

Plastic pots have several holes in the base; no crocks are needed and peat-based or environmentally friendly compost is used in them.

Clay pots are preferred by many houseplant enthusiasts as their texture and colour are natural and do not clash with plants. They are, unfortunately, less widely available than plastic and are easily broken.

Plastic pots are available in many colours, including green, white, yellow and black. They are light and cheap and readily available, but lack the aesthetic appeal of clay and are best hidden in containers.

Houseplants in either clay or plastic pots can be given a more attractive setting when placed in a cache pot. Select a cache pot to suit the plant in shape, colouring and materials, as well as its surroundings.

SUCCESSFUL REPOTTING

When a houseplant fills its pot with roots it is essential to move it into a larger one. If left, growth is stunted and the plant deteriorates. Repotting provides the plant with further nutrients and more space for its roots. It also creates a firmer base for the plant, balancing leaf growth and helping to prevent it falling over. At each repotting, move the plant into a pot only slightly larger, especially during its early life (*see page 15 for details*). In a pot that is too large, the plant is surrounded by too much compost and its roots can become saturated with water which eventually causes them to decay and the plant to die. Very large plants have the top layer of their compost replaced instead of repotting.

HOW TO RECOGNIZE A POT-BOUND PLANT

The clearest indication that repotting is needed is when the plant's roots are growing out of the pot's base. There are other, less obvious, signs, including a general lack of vigour and deterioration in health, caused by the plant being deprived of nutrients. New leaves are small and old ones become increasingly pale and yellow. Also, pot-bound flowering plants produce fewer flowers.

LEFT If a plant is thought to be pot-bound, carefully remove the pot and inspect the roots. If the compost is dry, the pot easily lifts off the soil-ball. However, if the pot resists, (see below) for advice on its removal. If the outside of the soil-ball is smothered with small, fibrous roots, repotting is essential; if only partly covered, replace the pot and gently water the compost.

2 Inspect the roots and, when repotting a plant in a clay pot, remove the crock (broken piece of clay pot) from the soil-ball's base. Tease out the roots: it may be necessary to use a stiff label.

New leaves are smaller than normal, with pale areas between the veins. They are also likely to hang limply due to lack of moisture.

Stems become thin and weak.

Compost may be dry and crusty, an indication that it is unable to retain sufficient moisture. Neglected plants are frequently pot-bound.

Roots in search of moisture and nutrients grow out of a pot's base when the compost is completely exhausted and the pot is too full of roots.

Pot-bound plant before repotting.

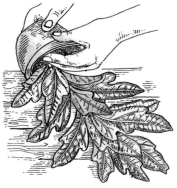

1 Thoroughly water the plant the day before repotting it. Remove the pot by placing fingers over the top of the soil-ball and inverting the pot. Hold the pot and tap its rim on a firm surface (*above*). The soil-ball will usually come out of the pot. If it resists, run a knife between the soil-ball and pot to loosen the roots.

3 Select a clean pot, slightly larger than the present one – see page 15 for the correct size increases. When repotting into a plastic pot, there is no need to place a small piece of broken clay pot in the pot's base. However, when using a clay pot it is usual to add one (*see right*).

4 Place and firm a handful of compost in the pot's base and position the soil-ball on top. Check that its surface is below the rim, so that the compost can be adequately watered. This distance varies according to the pot's size (*see right* for the recommended spaces). If the distance is too small, insufficient water will be given when the plant is watered.

When the plant is correctly positioned, trickle and gently firm new compost around the old soil-ball. Do not ram the compost too tightly into the pot.

5 If necessary, add further compost and gently firm it, leaving the recommended space at the top for watering. Finally, gently tap the side of the pot to level the surface. Then, stand the plant where surplus moisture can drain freely and gently trickle water on top of the compost. Completely fill the watering space. Allow surplus water to drain, later placing the pot in an attractive outer container. Do not water the compost again until it shows signs of becoming dry – the surface assumes a light colouring.

REPOTTING NOTEBOOK

✳ When repotting, use either a combination of plastic pots and peat-based compost, or clay pots and loam-based compost, depending on the plant's requirements.

✳ Pots are available in sizes from 6–38cm (2½in–15in) wide, but only five sizes are usually needed: 6–8cm (2½in–3½in), 13cm (5in), 18cm (7in) and 25cm (10in). When repotting, always use only the next size up.

✳ When potting and repotting, leave sufficient space between the compost's surface and rim to allow plants to be watered effectively. This space needs to increase in proportion to the pot's size: for 6–13cm (2½–5in) wide pots, leave 12mm (½in); 14–19cm (5½–7½in) leave 18mm (¾in); 20–23cm (8–9in) leave 2.5cm (1in); and 25–30cm (10–12in) leave 36mm (1½in).

✳ Soak clay pots for 24 hours before using them so that they do not draw water from the potting compost.

Using a clay pot

Use loam-based compost, formed of loam, sharp sand, moist peat and fertilizers.

Leave space so that the compost can be properly watered. For the gap needed, see Repotting Notebook (above).

Place a small crock (concave side downwards) over the drainage hole.

Put a handful of compost into the pot's base, covering the crock.

A healthy, recently repotted plant soon resumes growth, producing young shoots and fresh, brightly coloured leaves.

After repotting, place the plant in light shade until growth restarts. This is indicated by the development of fresh shoots. Until then, keeping the plant out of strong and direct sunlight ensures that the need for water is reduced.

Position plants with variegated leaves in good light, so that their colours are enhanced. Strong sunlight, however, should be avoided.

Plants with uniform outlines should be rotated about 90 degrees several times a week. If not, leaves turn towards the light.

Place the plastic or clay pot in an ornamental outer pot (often called a cache or display pot). Select a colour that harmonizes with the plant.

Healthy plant after repotting.

WATERING AND FEEDING

Without water, plants soon die. But they also deteriorate when given too much moisture; compost becomes swamped and airless and roots suffocate and die. The aim of watering is to provide plants with adequate water at the times they need it. During summer, houseplants need more water than in winter, although the compost of winter-flowering houseplants must be kept moist.

Most plants are watered by moistening the compost (*see below*), but tillandsias and air plants are mist-sprayed (soaking their leaves in water), while bromeliads that form urns are mainly watered by filling the urns with water.

Houseplants underachieve if not fed regularly once they have filled their pot with roots. Therefore, regular feeding is essential (*see on page 17*). While small, houseplants can be repotted into a larger pot (*see page 14–15*), but large, floor-standing plants are too big for this treatment. Instead, they are top dressed (*see page 17*).

JUDGING WHEN WATER IS NEEDED

The need for water can be assessed in several ways; tapping clay pots and rubbing the compost's surface are traditional ways, while moisture-meters and indicator strips are more recent. However, with experience it is often possible to judge if a plant needs water just by looking at the compost; if dark it is moist, but a light colour indicates that water is needed.

ABOVE Tapping clay pots with a cotton-reel attached to a cane is a well-known method: a dull note indicates moist compost, while a ring tells that water is needed.

LEFT Moisture-meters are increasing in popularity; by inserting a thin, pencil-like probe into compost the amount of moisture present is indicated on a dial. It is an efficient way to assess the presence of moisture, but repeated insertions of the probe eventually damage roots. Nevertheless, it is an ideal way for a novice to gain experience of when a houseplant needs water.

ABOVE Rubbing a thumb on the surface of compost is a popular way to assess the presence of moisture. Only add water when the compost is dry and has lost its sponginess. However, repeated pressings compact compost and eventually exclude air.

ABOVE Moisture-indicator strips (also known as watering signals) can be inserted and left in compost. They indicate when the compost is dry and thereby take much of the guesswork out of deciding when water is needed.

APPLYING WATER

The most popular way to water houseplants is by slowly dribbling water from a watering-can directly on the compost. This is known as 'over the rim' watering. At each application of water, fill the complete area between the compost's surface and the pot's rim. An alternative way is to stand pots in a bowl of water until moisture seeps to the compost's surface. Then, remove the pot and allow excess water to drain.

When a houseplant is in a large pot and cannot be repotted the compost needs to be top dressed every spring. This involves removing the top 25–36mm (1–1½ in) of old compost and replacing it with fresh. Take care not to damage the plant's roots. Leave a gap between the top of the compost and the pot's rim, so that the plant can be watered.

FEEDING HOUSEPLANTS

Plants need a balanced diet to remain healthy and to create an attractive display. Both foliage and summer-flowering houseplants are normally fed at ten- to fourteen-day intervals from early spring to late summer. Winter-flowering houseplants are fed at the same frequency while they remain in flower.

ABOVE The most popular way to feed houseplants is by diluting and mixing a concentrated liquid fertilizer in clean tepid water. Adhere to the strength recommended by the manufacturer. Before applying the fertilizer, ensure that the compost is moist so that it will be quickly and evenly absorbed.

Make up just enough fertilizer to feed your plants on each occasion and do not store any surplus. Keep in one container for fertilizer and do not use it for anything else. Store all chemicals safely.

Using feeding sticks and pills is a clean and quick way to feed houseplants. Feeding sticks (above) are gently pushed into compost, about 12mm (½ in) from the pot's side. Pills (below) are also inserted into compost. Some devices enable pills to be inserted without having to dirty hands on compost. Both feeding sticks and pills provide plants with food over a long period, but they encourage roots to become congested around them.

Do not use feeding sticks and pills after mid-summer for plants that flower through-out summer. The fertilizer released will last for the rest of the flowering season and plants will be able to become dormant after this period. Use on winter-flowering plants in autumn and early winter.

SAVING A PLANT IN DRY COMPOST

When watering is neglected, plants wilt and eventually die. During the period a plant is wilting, there is a point when however much water is subsequently given it will not recover. This is known as the permanent wilting point. However, most plants can be revived if watered soon enough.

Stand the pot in a bowl with about 36mm (1½ in) of water in it. Cut off faded flowers and if the leaves are smooth mist-spray them (*above*). When moisture rises to the compost's surface, remove and place in light shade for a few days.

SAVING A PLANT IN WATERLOGGED COMPOST

If compost becomes totally saturated with water, air is excluded and roots cease to function. The plant wilts, leaves become limp and eventually slime covers the compost. If this state is noticed early enough, plants can be saved successfully.

1 Invert the pot and plant and place a hand under the soil-ball (*below left*). Tap the pot's rim on the corner of a hard surface, so that the soil-ball slips out. Remove crocks from the soil-ball's base.

2 Wrap several pieces of absorbent kitchen towel around the soil-ball to soak up water (*above*). Check that root mealy bugs (like small woodlice) are not present. If they are, pick off and after the plant has been repotted use an insecticide. Leave the soil-ball wrapped in absorbent paper until it is lightly dry (*below*). If the soil-ball is packed with roots, leave it fully exposed to the air.

3 When the soil-ball's surface is dry – but not crumbly – repot the plant into a clean pot, using fresh compost. Leave the plant for a few days and then water the compost. Do not place the plant in strong sunlight until it has fully recovered.

GROOMING AND CARE

Unless regularly groomed, many houseplants become dirty or grow a mass of tangled shoots that dramatically reduce their attractiveness. Dust radically diminishes the ability of leaves to function and create growth. It blocks breathing pores (stoma) and reduces the amount of light reaching growth-activating cells within the leaves.

If large, smooth-surfaced leaves are covered with a thick layer of dirt, use a soft cloth to dust it off lightly before wiping with water. And never place plants in strong sunlight before moisture dries from them; small water droplets act as lenses and intensify the sun's rays, thereby burning leaves and causing them to dry and become brown.

Clean, non-chalky soft water is ideal for cleaning leaves (rainwater or tap water that has been boiled, in areas of hard water); although milk, beer and dilute vinegar are also recommended, they do little to shine leaves. Olive oil is also advocated, but retains dust which damages leaves. Several proprietary leaf-cleaning substances are available.

LOOKING AFTER LEAVES

Many plants are grown specifically for their attractive leaves. If they become dirty or damaged, this diminishes the display. Cleaning leaves is therefore important and the method of doing this depends on their size and texture. Damaged leaves can be cut out, together with long and misplaced shoots.

When vigorous stems spoil the shape of a plant, use sharp scissors to cut them back to just above a leaf-joint. Azaleas often develop long shoots that are best removed.

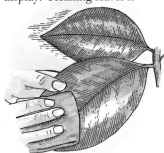

Wipe large, smooth-surfaced leaves with a damp cloth (above). These include rubber plants (*Ficus elastica*) and Swiss cheese plant (*Monstera deliciosa*). Plants with masses of smooth-surfaced leaves can be inverted and dipped in a bowl of clean water (left). Some plants have hairy leaves and these are best cleaned carefully using a soft brush (right).

Cut out dead leaves, but avoid leaving small snags that will die back. If dead leaves are at the top of a shoot (above), these are best removed by using sharp scissors to cut the stem back to its base.

TRAINING AND SUPPORTING

Climbing plants need support to prevent stems sprawling, becoming tangled and intruding on their neighbours. Split canes and plastic-mesh frameworks are ideal for climbing foliage plants, but pink jasmine (*Jasminum polyanthum*) has more eye-appeal when supported with loops of pliable canes or proprietary supports that hook on pots and form a loop 30–38cm (12–15in) high. When stems are about 30cm (12in) long, insert the supports and curl shoots around them.

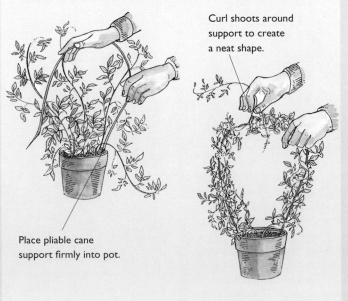

Curl shoots around support to create a neat shape.

Place pliable cane support firmly into pot.

LOOKING
AFTER FLOWERS

Flowering houseplants need regular attention when they are in bloom. If they are neglected, dead flowers remain on the plant, and this can encourage the presence of diseases. Also, removing faded flowers extends the flowering period by prompting further buds to form. Sometimes, the flower and its stalk are removed.

ABOVE Most dead flowers on houseplants are picked off individually and placed on a compost heap. Azaleas produce a profusion of flowers over several weeks; as the first ones fade, hold the shoot and carefully pinch them off.

ABOVE When dead-heading cyclamen, pull off each faded flower together with its stem. Hold the stem firmly and give it a sharp tug. It will separate from the plant's base. If just the flower is removed, the stem slowly decays and encourages other flowers and stems to decay. It also looks unsightly. Place the flowers and stems on a compost heap; do not leave them at the plant's base.

HOLIDAY CARE

Many houseplants are lovingly looked after throughout the year, only to deteriorate or die through neglect when you are away on holiday. Neighbours often act as plant-sitters, but unless the person has experience of looking after plants it is likely that they will be either starved of moisture or excessively watered. Both could cause their death.

Instead of relying on a plant-sitter, automatic watering devices can be constructed (*see below and at right*).

A few days before going away, remove flowers that would have faded by the time of your return. Also, cut off damaged leaves, especially if soft and furry.

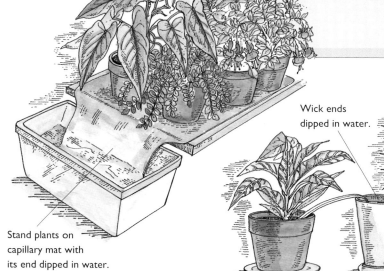

Stand plants on capillary mat with its end dipped in water.

If plants are large they are best left in their saucers, moved into the centre of a lightly shaded room and placed on a large polythene sheet. During the week before going on holiday, water the compost several times. If the holiday is only for a week or ten days, preparing them in this way is usually sufficient to keep them healthy.

A WICK WATERER

Most capillary and wick methods of watering involve grouping plants together, perhaps on a draining board or next to each other so that wicks can be trailed between them. This is ideal during vacations, but not practical at other times. However, a simple wick-watering device that is more pleasing to the eye is created by positioning a plant on top of a water reservoir.

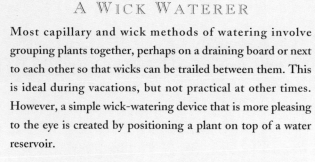

Push a wick into compost in a pot, ensuring both are in close contact.

Pass the lower part of the wick through a hole in a small, waterproof pot and trail it into water. Cut a further hole in the container so that the water can be topped up.

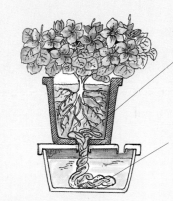

Wick ends dipped in water.

When looking after small plants, they can be placed in large trays with 12mm (½ in) of water in their base. This will keep them alive for two weeks, especially if positioned in light shade.

Another way is to place a capillary mat on a draining board and to trail one end in a sink filled with water. Alternatively, trail the end in a bowl of water. Stand plants on the matting. This system works best when plants are in plastic pots filled with peat-based compost and without crocks in their base.

A further method is to stand a pot of water on an inverted saucer and to trail wicks (with their ends in the water) into the compost.

SOWING SEEDS

Growing your own plants, whether from seed or by one of the vegetative means (*see pages 24–31*) is immensely satisfying. Of the many plants that can be raised from seed it could be best to begin with flowering annuals. Most seeds are available only in fairly large quantities, but you cannot have too many summer-flowering busy Lizzies (*Impatiens*) and butterfly plants (*Schizanthus*), black-eyed Susan (*Thunbergia*) and slipper flowers (*Calceolaria*) – and, if you find you have, there will be no problem in finding homes for the spares. Few houseplant annuals are generally available as bought plants and it is certainly much cheaper to raise your own.

Next there are the short-lived pot plants such as Chinese primrose (*Primula sinensis*) and fairy primrose (*P. malacoides*), which give extra pleasure at reduced cost when you have raised them yourself from seed. Then move on to the rarer plants such as some of the cacti and succulents, and once you have started to raise these you will be hooked.

To grow plants from seed you must be able to provide somewhere where seed trays can be kept in warmth at a fairly constant temperature, in good light, undisturbed and away from draughts. When you pot up seedlings their pots will take up quite a bit of room. But little equipment is needed and you certainly do not need a greenhouse – a sunny spare room or even a kitchen windowsill is ideal.

GETTING STARTED
Some suitable seeds for houseplants are on sale in garden centres or can be ordered from the seed merchants' catalogues. Others may have to be obtained from specialists. Horticultural societies, gardening clubs and the gardening magazines can help you to locate sources for more unusual plants.

Use small trays, known as seed pans, for small quantities of seeds and standard seed trays for larger quantities. Keep each container for seeds of one species only as the plants grow at different rates. Do not mix seeds within the tray as some are bound to grow faster than others. Use plastic labels and waterproof ink to label the trays.

1 Place a layer of peat or peat substitute in the tray. (If using a clay tray, first soak it for 24 hours and line it with small, clean, broken pot pieces.) Top with seed compost, which is light and sterile and contains well-balanced nutrients at the correct strength. Firm in the compost gently, carefully packing it into the corners and all round the edges.

2 Add more compost to fill the tray completely. Smooth and level the surface by passing a straight piece of wood over it. Firm the compost down, with the flat of your hand, a jam jar or a convenient piece of wood cut to the right size. When firmed the compost should come to about 18mm (¾ in) below the edge of the tray.

3 Fold a piece of paper in half and pour the seeds into the 'V'. By tapping the edge of the paper gently you can spread the seeds more finely and evenly over the surface of the compost. Avoid sprinkling the seeds too close to the edges as the compost dries out quickly there.

Label the tray with the name of the plant and the date.

SUITABLE PLANTS
TO GROW FROM SEED

Annuals, pot plants, foliage plants (marked *) and flowering houseplants: *Calceolaria* × *herbeohybrida* (slipper flower); *Campanula isophylla* (Italian bellflower); *Capsicum annuum* (Christmas pepper); *Chrysanthemum* species (chrysanthemum); *Coleus* hybrids (coleus*); *Cyclamen persicum* (cyclamen); *Datura cornigera* (angel's trumpet); *Freesia* hybrids (freesia); *Impatiens walleriana* (busy Lizzie); *Kalanchoe blossfeldiana* (flaming Katy); *Lapageria rosea* (Chilean bellflower); *Musa* species (banana plant*); *Phoenix dactylifera* (palms* such as date palm); primroses, such as *Primula acaulis*, *P. sinensis* and *P. malacoides*; *Saintpaulia ionantha* (African violet); *Schizanthus pinnatus* (butterfly flower); *Sinningia speciosa* (gloxinia); *Solanum capsicastrum* (winter cherry); *Thunbergia alata* (black-eyed Susan).

4 Almost all seeds germinate better when covered with a thin layer of compost (check the seed packet for details). Sprinkle a fine layer of compost over the surface by passing it through a sieve. The layer should be three or four times the diameter of the seeds. Only the finest sprinkling is needed for very small seeds.

6 If you do not use a propagator you can slide the seed tray into a polythene bag, and tie loosely with a tag. Alternatively, cover the top with a sheet of glass, making sure that it does not actually touch the compost. Remove the glass or polythene every day and wipe off the condensation before replacing it.

DAILY CARE

Check the compost every day, without disturbing the tray. Water it from below as before when necessary, to keep it constantly moist but not wet. Keep the trays in a draught-free place and at an even temperature. If there is no specific recommendation on the packet, maintain at between 16–21°C (61–70°F).

For seeds that germinate best in the dark, keep in a cupboard or place a folded newspaper over the glass or propagator lid until the seedlings appear. As soon as this happens give the seedlings good light (but not strong sunlight) and remove the glass cover or polythene bag or open the ventilators of the propagator to allow fresh air in. Remove the cover altogether as seedlings grow.

When the seedlings are large enough to handle, they should be pricked out.

5 Next, water the compost by standing the tray in a dish of water, filled so that the water comes half way up the sides of the tray. Leave the tray in the container until water appears on the surface of the compost. This ensures that the compost is evenly wet. Remove the tray and allow it to drain so that there is no excess water in the compost.

If your seed tray is part of a propagator place the lid over the tray. Leave the cover on the tray until seedlings appear.

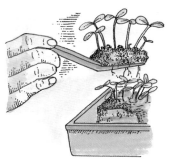

1 As soon as the seedlings are big enough to be handled, transfer them to another tray to give them more growing space.

First prepare a tray of compost and firm it as before. Have ready a wad of wet newspaper on which to stand the seedlings so that their tiny roots do not dry out.

Use a plant label or a fork (a plastic picnic fork is ideal) to 'dig' up small clumps of seedlings. When separating the seedlings, do not handle their roots, which are very easily damaged, but hold them gently by their leaves.

2 With a pencil or small dibber make holes in the new compost, spaced 4–5cm (1.5–2in) apart. Drop the seedlings into the holes one by one, handling them gently, and firm them in with their seed 'leaves' just above the compost surface. Water from below and allow to drain as before. Keep the tray in very bright light (but not strong sun). True leaves will develop as the seedlings grow. Pot plants into individual pots when their leaves show signs of beginning to touch.

TAKING CUTTINGS

New plants can be grown from cuttings, by dividing the roots, or by growing on small plantlets and offsets produced by the parent plant. These are known as vegetative means of propagation. When growing plants from seed you cannot always be sure exactly what the results will be, as, except with F_1 hybrids, nature is free to choose some of the details such as exact flower colour or markings. In vegetative propagation you are reproducing the parent plant exactly, so that you get a miniature replica of it.

Propagating plants from cuttings can be a very good way to grow replacements for short-lived plants and much-loved plants which are outgrowing their space. It can also, of course, be an ideal way to increase the numbers of favourite plants of which you would like more. By way of equipment you need nothing more than clean flower pots, a sharp knife, cuttings compost, which is well aerated and well draining but also moisture retentive, a polythene bag and a few short sticks to support it. Mist sprays, hormone rooting powder and propagating units are optional extras, and you must provide a light place with an even temperature 13–18°C (55–64°F), or more for tropical plants. Steps 1–4 below show how several cuttings can be grown in one pot.

TIP CUTTINGS
Select a healthy specimen with plenty of well-developed stems, taken from the outside of the plant. Soft new growth does not readily root. Water the plant well the day before taking cuttings.

2 Trim the stem, cutting it off just below the bottom of the leaf-joint (the point from which new roots develop.) Cleanly slice off the lower leaf or pairs of leaves. If preparing several cuttings keep in water until all are ready.

3 With a dibber or pencil, make a hole in a pot of compost. Dip the cutting in rooting powder. Insert it in the compost, making sure the leaves are not touching it.

4 Water the compost from above. To conserve moisture make a 'tent' around the cutting with a polythene bag (with holes for air) supported on split canes.

1 Use a sharp knife or craft knife to cut a 7.5–13cm (3–5in) length of stem, with a growing tip at the end. Make the cut just above a leaf joint, and cut it at an angle sloping away from the joint.

CARING FOR THE CUTTINGS

Keep the cuttings in good light (but not direct sun) and steady warmth until new growth indicates that roots have formed. Then remove polythene and pot the plants on in potting compost. Pinch them out at the growing points as they grow to encourage bushy growth.

STEM CUTTINGS

Plants, such as ivy, which have long, trailing, woody stems with leaves growing along their length can be propagated from stem cuttings taken from a length of stem, without growing tips on the individual cuttings. One long piece of stem is divided into several cuttings.

1 Cut off a good length of young, supple stem, using a sharp knife (*above*). Cutting just above the leaf joints, divide the stems into small pieces, each with a leaf.

2 Insert the cuttings into a pot of cuttings compost, several to a pot, using a pencil or dibber to make the holes (*above*). Avoid placing the cuttings too close to the edges of the pot where compost quickly becomes dry.

ROOTING CUTTINGS IN WATER

African violet leaf petiole cuttings can be rooted in water, as can other soft petiole cuttings and stem cuttings of busy Lizzies, pelargoniums and other plants. To ensure that the cutting cannot slip into the water, use a bottle or narrow-necked jar and cover the top with kitchen paper, held in place with a rubber band.

Pierce a hole in the paper and insert the cutting. Keep it in a warm, light, draught-free place, making sure that the end remains in water, until roots develop. Then tear away the paper, remove the cutting and pot it up in a small pot.

3 Water the pot, then cover with a 'tent' of polythene as before, making sure that the leaves do not touch the polythene (*above*). When small new leaves appear (*below*) the cuttings have rooted and should be transferred to separate small pots of potting compost.

LEAF PETIOLE CUTTINGS

A leaf petiole cutting uses a leaf and its leaf-stalk (the petiole). Soft-stemmed plants root particularly well in this way and the method is often used for African violets. Whereas stem and tip cuttings often root without hormone rooting powder, leaf petiole cuttings root more reliably if it is used.

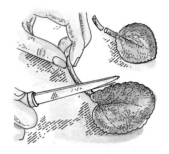

1 Choose a plant that has plenty of leaves, and make sure that the leaves you select for cuttings have firm, fleshy petioles. Cut off leaf-stalks at the base, using a sharp knife and taking them evenly from around the plant.

Handling the cuttings with great care, and holding them by the leaf, trim down the stems so that they are about 36mm (1½in) long.

2 Dip the petiole tips in hormone rooting powder (*above*) and insert the cuttings in a pot of cuttings compost, using a dibber or pencil to make the holes. Firm in the cuttings (*below*) and water the compost from below by standing the pot in water, to make sure the leaves do not get wet. Put the pot in a polythene 'tent' as in step 3 (*left*) and keep it in a warm place until new growth appears.

INCREASING CACTI AND OTHER SUCCULENTS

Succulent plants are popular and once established are ideal for brightening sunny windowsills throughout the year. Indeed, they tolerate extremes of temperature better than any other type of plant. Many of these plants can be raised from seeds and are sold in mixtures or individual species. But a much quicker way to produce replicas of a plant you like is to grow new plants from cuttings.

There are various ways of taking cuttings of succulent plants. One method is that used for mother-in-law's tongue (*Sansevieria trifasciata* also known as snake plant and good luck plant) where a leaf is cut into sections; with other plants whole leaves are rooted, while cacti are grown from short stubs.

Take care when detaching leaves that the mother plant's shape is not ruined; a few leaves removed from the back of a plant usually does no harm and passes unnoticed.

LEAF DIVISION

Large plants can be easily increased by dividing the soil-ball and roots, which is essential to perpetuate the yellow-edged markings on *Sansevieria trifasciata* 'Laurentii' (*see page 32*). The normal species can be increased by cutting stems or leaves into pieces.

1 Choose a healthy plant and use a sharp knife to sever one or two leaves at their base. Do not take them from one position, as this will mar the plant's shape. Water the plant a few days before severing the leaves. Flaccid leaves do not readily root.

2 Place the leaf on a flat surface and use a sharp knife to cut it into pieces about 5cm (2in) deep (*above*). Avoid creating torn surfaces, as they do not readily root.

3 Fill and firm a shallow but wide pot with equal parts moist peat and sharp sand. Form a slit with a knife, then push a cutting about 18mm (3/4in) into it (*above*). Ensure the cutting is the right way up. Lightly water the compost and place in gentle warmth.

SMALL AND CIRCULAR LEAVES

Several succulent plants have small, circular and relatively flat leaves. These include *Sedum sieboldii*, widely known in North America as the October plant and October daphne, and its variegated form 'Medio-variegatum'. These are easily increased in spring and early summer by pressing leaves into the surface of well-drained compost formed of equal parts moist peat and sharp sand. Use a sharp knife or scissors to cut off entire stems, rather than removing a few leaves from several shoots. Do not take too many stems from one plant.

1 Snap off the leaves, taking care not to squash them. Leave the surfaces to dry for a couple of days before using them as cuttings.

2 Press individual leaves on the compost's surface, then lightly water them. Place the pot in gentle warmth and light shade.

WHOLE-LEAF CUTTINGS

Some succulents, such as the jade plant (*Crassula argentea*, also known as dollar plant, cauliflower ears and Chinese rubber plant), have leaves that can be removed and inserted vertically into well-drained compost. They are best removed and encouraged to root in spring and early summer. High temperatures are not necessary to initiate rooting.

1 Select a healthy, well-watered plant and gently snap off leaves by bending them downwards (*above*). They should snap off close to the main stem and not leave short spurs. Leave each cutting exposed to air for a couple of days before inserting in compost.

2 Fill a clean pot with equal parts moist peat and sharp sand and firm it to about 12mm (½ in) below the rim. Use a small dibber or knife to form a hole 18mm (¾ in) deep and insert a cutting in it. Firm compost around it (*above*). Put several cuttings in one pot. Water the compost and place in light shade and gentle warmth.

CACTUS CUTTINGS

Most cacti are known for their prickly nature, but this should not stop cuttings being taken. If necessary, wear a pair of thin rubber kitchen gloves. Cacti that create a mass of small stems from around their base are easily increased from cuttings. Mammillarias, the peanut cactus (*Chamaecereus silvestrii*) and lobivias are some of the cacti that can be increased in this way.

1 Use a sharp knife to remove well-formed young stems from around the outside of the clump (*above*). Sever the stems directly at their base, so that unsightly short stubs of growth are not left on the mother plant. Do not take them all from the same position to avoid spoiling the plant's appearance.

   Leave the cuttings (*below*) for a couple of days so that their ends can dry before inserting in cactus compost. This enables them to root much more quickly than if inserted immediately after being severed.

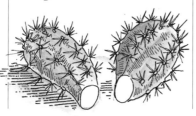

AVOID HIGH TEMPERATURES

It is often thought that high temperatures are essential to encourage cuttings of cacti and other succulents to develop roots. Gentle warmth and light shade are much better, as the cutting does not then become dehydrated before roots develop. Do not position pots of cuttings on sunny, unshaded windowsills.

2 Fill a small pot with equal parts moist peat and sharp sand and firm it to 12mm (½ in) below the rim. Sprinkle a thin layer of sharp sand on the surface and use a small dibber to make a hole about 2.5cm (1in) deep, into which a cutting can be inserted. Firm compost around its base. Lightly water the compost.

Place cuttings in gentle warmth and light shade. Rooting takes a few weeks in spring and early summer.

LEAF CUTTINGS

This is a form of vegetative propagation and involves detaching leaves from a parent plant and encouraging roots to form on them. Some leaf cuttings are taken from whole leaves, while others are cut into squares, triangles or cross-sections. Early to mid-summer is the best time to encourage roots to form on leaves, thereby ensuring that young plants are well established by autumn.

Before severing a leaf, water the parent plant thoroughly and several times, preferably during the previous day. This ensures that the leaf is full of water and will not deteriorate before roots have formed. Also, check that the leaf is healthy, free from pests and diseases and a good example of the parent plant. Each leaf used as a cutting should be relatively young and without surfaces that have become hard and old. These do not root rapidly.

After the cuttings have been taken and inserted in compost, position them out of strong and direct sunlight; small leaf-squares and triangles soon shrivel when in strong sunlight. Indeed, it is better to place them on a cool, well-shaded windowsill than on a sunny one. Keep the compost moist during the rooting period and as soon as roots and shoots develop, remove the plastic covering and lower the temperature.

WHOLE-LEAF CUTTINGS
Plants such as the rex begonia (*Begonia rex*), iron-cross begonia (*B. masoniana*) and Cape primrose (*Streptocarpus × hybridus*) can be increased from whole-leaf cuttings. Choose relatively young leaves.

1 Sever the leaf-stalk of a healthy leaf close to its base (*above*), taking care not to leave a short snag on the plant that later would die back.

Then, place the severed leaf upside down on a wooden board and cut off the leaf-stalk, close to the leaf.

2 Use a sharp knife to make cuts, 12–25mm (½–1in) apart, across the main and secondary veins (*above*), but taking care not to cut completely through the leaf.

3 Place the leaf vein-side downwards on equal parts moist peat and sharp sand. Use small stones (*above*) or pieces of U-shaped wire, inserted astride the veins, to hold the leaf in close contact with the compost.

4 Lightly water the compost, allow excess moisture to evaporate from the leaf's surface and then cover with a transparent lid. Place in gentle warmth and light shade. Roots develop from the cut veins and young shoots from the surface. As soon as the young plants are large enough to handle, transfer them into individual pots.

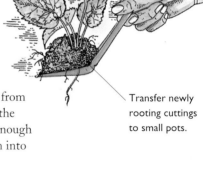

Transfer newly rooting cuttings to small pots.

HORIZONTAL LEAF-SQUARES

As well as being inserted vertically into compost, small leaf-squares can be pressed flat on the surface of compost formed of equal parts moist peat and sharp sand. These leaf cuttings are about 30mm (1¼in) square and they need to be carefully secured horizontally on the compost's surface. Because they are small, hooked pieces of wire are much easier to use compared to pebbles.

Leaf-squares

These are square and many more can be created from an individual leaf than the triangular type (SEE FAR BELOW). After severing a leaf from a healthy plant, cut off its leaf-stalk and place on a board. First, cut the leaf into strips about 30mm (1¼in) wide, with a main or secondary vein down the middle. Then, cut each strip into squares (BELOW LEFT). Each square is inserted separately and by about one-third of its depth into equal parts moist peat and sharp sand. It is vital that cuttings are inserted with the side that was nearest to the leafstalk facing downwards (BELOW RIGHT).

After forming a slit with a knife and inserting a cutting, firm compost around it, lightly water the surface and place in gentle warmth and light shade. Cover with a plastic, translucent lid.

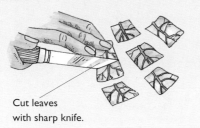

Cut leaves with sharp knife.

Insert cuttings in compost.

Leaf-sections

The Cape primrose (*Streptocarpus × hybridus*) can be increased by severing leaves into sections, in addition to positioning whole-leaf cuttings on the surface of compost (*see page 26*). This is best performed in early or mid-summer.

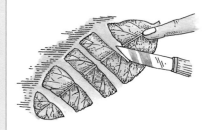

Sever a healthy leaf and place it on a flat board. Use a sharp knife to cut it laterally into pieces about 5cm (2in) deep *(above)*.

Use the blade of a knife to form 18mm (¾in) deep slits in the compost, into which cuttings can be inserted and firmed.

Leaf-triangles

These are triangular and easier to insert in compost than leaf-squares. They also tend to be slightly larger and this gives them a greater reserve of food while they are developing their roots.

1 Water a mother plant and during the following day remove a healthy leaf; sever it close to the plant's base and then again next to the leaf. Place the leaf on a flat board and use a sharp knife to cut triangles, each with its point towards the position where the stalk joined it.

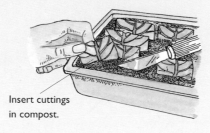

2 Fill and firm a seed tray with equal parts moist peat and sharp sand. Use a knife to make slits into which cuttings can be inserted to half their depth. Firm compost around them and place in light shade and gentle warmth.

3 When the cuttings have developed plantlets, transfer them into small, individual pots. Water the compost and place in light shade until established.

The leaves of the Cape primrose (*Streptocarpus × hybridus*) can be used to propagate this plant. Large, healthy leaves should be used.

RUNNERS AND PLANTLETS

Many houseplants obligingly produce plantlets or offsets from which new plants can be grown. Some send out runners or stolons (creeping stems), which, in the wild, travel along the ground, developing a series of tiny new plants that take root in the soil. Others develop roots along their arching stems, wherever these touch the ground. The runners or stems can be pegged down into the ground along their length to encourage rooting. In houseplants stolons and their little plantlets can be an attractive feature of the plant and they are usually left to hang decoratively from the plant.

Other plants produce their plantlets around, and attached to, the parent plant, and these miniature plants, usually known as offsets, can be detached and grown on. Some plantlets begin to produce their own roots while hanging on the plant, while others develop them when they come in contact with a suitable growing medium.

LAYERING

Propagating from runners and arching stems is known as layering. Ivies and other climbing plants can easily be reproduced in this way. As this method of propagation produces a replica of the parent plant, a healthy parent is essential. Water the plant well the day before.

1 Fill a pot with cuttings compost and firm down the compost so that the top is about 12mm (^{1}/2in) below the rim. Place the pot next to the parent plant.

Fold over a stem (without cutting it off) near a leaf-joint, about 15cm (6in) from the tip, to form a V in the stem.

2 Use bent wire to anchor the 'V' of the stem into the compost. Firm compost over the 'V' and water the compost from above.

3 Keep the compost moist as new roots develop. When fresh growth appears at the tip of the stem, this indicates that roots have formed; sever the new plant from its parent with a sharp knife or scissors.

AERIAL ROOTS

Climbing plants such as sweetheart vine (*Philodendron scandens*) produce aerial roots along their stems, and new plants can be grown from these by the same layering method. (For convenience you may wish to stand the parent plant and the pot for the new plant in a plastic tray.) Untie a stem of the parent plant and peg it into a pot of compost as before, about 2.5cm (1in) deep. When there is new growth, sever the stem to separate the plants.

Other plants for layering include kangaroo vine (*Cissus antarctica*), devil's ivy (*Epipremnum aureum* or *Scindapsus aureus*), Swedish ivy (*Plectranthus oertendahlii*), and grape ivy (*Rhoicissus rhomboidera* or *Cissus rhombifolia*).

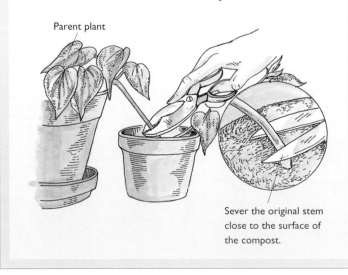

Parent plant

Sever the original stem close to the surface of the compost.

TRAILING OFFSETS

The spider plant (*Chlorophytum comosum*) is one of the easiest plants to grow from offsets, and mother of thousands (*Saxifraga stolonifera*) is another. Both produce small versions of themselves at the end of long, arching stems.

Stand the plant on a tray and surround it with several small pots filled with cuttings or potting compost. Water both the plant and the compost in the pots.

Arch the stolons over one by one so that the plantlets are resting on the surface of the compost, one per pot (*above*). Use a hairpin or a piece of bent wire to anchor each stolon in place.

Keep the compost moist, and sever the stolons when new growth appears to indicate that roots are well formed (*below*).

DETACHABLE OFFSETS

Other plants have offsets growing on the plant itself, either on the leaf surface or (more usually) around the rosettes of leaves that form the plant. With these plants the offsets can be severed from the parent plant and grown in separate pots.

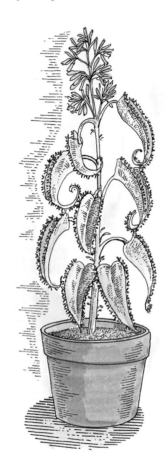

1 Typical plants with leaf offsets are chandelier plant (*Kalanchoe tubiflora*), in which the offsets grow at the tips of the leaves, and Mexican hat or devil's backbone (*Kalanchoe daigremontianum*), in which they grow around the leaf edges as shown above.

Offsets grow much more readily when they are taken from a turgid plant. Well before removing the offsets, water the plant.

2 Fill a 7.5cm (3in) pot with potting compost and water the compost.

When offsets are very small (*above*), they need little space at first, and several plantlets can be started off in the same pot. Use your fingers, or a pair of tweezers, to remove a few plantlets from each leaf (so as not to alter the appearance of the parent plant), handling them very carefully.

3 Arrange the plantlets on the surface of the compost, so that each has its own growing space. Keep the compost moist by watering from below. When the plants grow, roots will have formed and they should be potted in individual pots.

OTHER OFFSETS

Many succulent plants and bromeliads have offsets that grow on, or round the base of, the plant. Sometimes these are easily identifiable as small new plants, as in many of the cacti, and in other cases they seem to be inextricably linked to the the parent, as in many bromeliads. In either case the best time to remove these offsets is when you are repotting the plant. Cut them off with a very sharp clean knife, in the case of those growing up round the base trying to ensure that you get a bit of root too. Allow cactus offsets to dry for a few days before planting them in cactus compost, and plant other plants in potting compost straight away. Half fill the pot first and hold the plant with the roots in the pot while you trickle in more compost. Firm in and water from below.

AIR LAYERING

Indoors and in temperate countries, rubber plants (*ficus*) are the most popular plants increased by air layering. Other houseplants occasionally raised in this way are dieffenbachia, dracaena and monstera. Air layering is an ideal way to give a tall, leggy plant that has lost its lower leaves a new term of life. It involves encouraging roots to develop just below the lowest leaf; when these are established the stem is severed and the plant re-potted. The old root part need not be discarded as it can be encouraged to develop further shoots (*see page 31*).

This is not a rapid method of propagation but it always attracts attention. To see a stem covered in peat and wrapped in plastic is novel, but the Chinese used a system of air layering many centuries before the technique became known in Europe and North America. It also became popular in the tropics and subtropics and in the Indian sub-continent was known as gootee-layering and marcottage. The stems of trees and shrubs outdoors were slit and wrapped in soil with coir fibre used as a bandage. To keep the soil moist, a small earthenware or bamboo pot was suspended above it and a wick used to transfer moisture to the soil.

Healthy leaves at the top of a rubber plant (*Ficus elastica*).

Strong stem, not excessively old or twisted and kinked.

A rubber plant that has lost its lower leaves and unless air layered eventually will be too unsightly to be displayed.

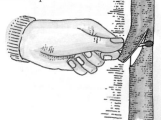

1 To ensure the plant is turgid, water the compost the day before air layering it. Use a sharp knife to make an upward-slanting cut, two-thirds through the stem and 7.5–10cm (3–4in) below the lowest leaf. At this stage, take care that the top of the plant does not bend and snap.

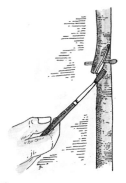

2 Use a matchstick to keep the surfaces of the cut apart. If they are allowed to close, the wound heals and does not readily develop roots. At this stage, the wound exudes latex (milky sap) which needs to be wiped away by using a damp cloth. Trim off the ends of the matchstick and use a small brush to coat the plant's cut surfaces with a hormone rooting powder. This encourages the rapid formation of roots. Use the tip of the brush to push the powder right inside the cut. Wash the brush immediately to remove the sap before it dries.

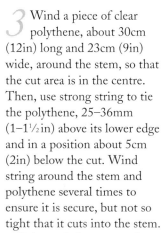

3 Wind a piece of clear polythene, about 30cm (12in) long and 23cm (9in) wide, around the stem, so that the cut area is in the centre. Then, use strong string to tie the polythene, 25–36mm (1–1½in) above its lower edge and in a position about 5cm (2in) below the cut. Wind string around the stem and polythene several times to ensure it is secure, but not so tight that it cuts into the stem.

Tying polythene around the stem in this way allows it to form a tube that can be filled with moist peat that encapsulates the cut area.

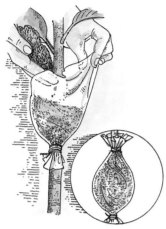

REJUVENATING AN OLD PLANT

After the top of an air-layered plant has been severed and re-potted, the old rooted part can be rejuvenated by using sharp secateurs to cut the stem back to just above dormant buds or small shoots. Keep the compost evenly moist but not saturated and place in gentle warmth and good light. Within a few weeks shoots will develop.

If a bushy plant is desired, leave all of the shoots intact, but to create a single stem remove all but the top one.

4 Carefully fill the polythene tube with moist peat, pushing it firmly – but without overly compacting it – around the stem. Fill the tube to within 7.5cm (3in) of the top of the polythene, then tie it securely around the stem; take care not to damage it.

6 Carefully remove the polythene and string and try to retain as much peat as possible around the roots. Loose peat, especially if dry, will fall from around them. Select a clean pot – usually about 13cm (5in) wide – for potting up the new plant.

BELOW Until the plant is firmly established, place it in light shade and away from draughts.

5 Place the plant in gentle warmth and light shade and every two weeks loosen the polythene at its top and check that the peat is still moist, but not waterlogged.

Within six to eight weeks, roots develop at the cut and can be seen through the clear polythene. While the roots are still white and before they begin to age and darken, use sharp secateurs to sever the stem immediately below the lower part of the polythene.

7 Put compost in the base of the pot and position the stem so that the roots will be covered by compost. Hold the stem upright and gently trickle compost around the roots. Spread them out and firm compost over and around them. Leave a gap of 12mm (½in) between the top of the compost and the rim of the pot. Gently but thoroughly water the compost. If the plant is unstable, initially support it with a cane.

Take care not to water the compost excessively while the roots are becoming established. Keeping the compost only lightly moist encourages faster root development and attractive foliage.

DIVISION AND CANE CUTTINGS

Division is an easy way to increase some congested houseplants and if they are not split into exceptionally small pieces there is an opportunity to produce several attractive plants instantly. Always use young, healthy pieces from around the outside of a clump; discard old parts from its centre. Houseplants that can be increased in this way include African violets (*Saintpaulia*), peace lily (*Spathiphyllum wallisii*), prayer plants (*Maranta*), cyperus, many ferns and mother-in-law's tongue (*Sansevieria*). Indeed, the only way to perpetuate the yellow edges on leaves of *Sansevieria trifasciata* 'Laurentii' is by division.

Cane cuttings are thick pieces of bare stem from plants with cane-like stems, such as yuccas and cordylines, cut into small lengths and either inserted vertically into or pressed on the surface of well-drained compost. They offer a good way to increase plants that are bare of leaves and so unattractive that otherwise they might have to be destroyed.

DIVISION

African violets (*Saintpaulia ionantha*) are easily increased by removing congested plants from their pots and teasing them apart. Tap the edge of a congested pot on a hard corner to remove the soil-ball (*above*). Gently pull the plants apart (*below*) and repot young pieces into small, individual pots. Water the compost.

1 Mother-in-law's tongue (*Sansevieria trifasciata* 'Laurentii') eventually fills its pot with fibrous roots; many stems and leaves arise directly from the roots. When the soil-ball is saturated with roots, the quality of the plant's leaves deteriorates. At that stage, divide the plant. Water the compost the day before dividing it. This ensures roots, stems and leaves are full of moisture. Dehydrated plants are less likely to survive division than those that have been well-watered.

2 Invert the plant and knock the pot's rim on a corner of a hard surface. As you ease out the plant, support the soil-ball, so that it gently slides from the pot but does not break up or fall on the floor.

Using your fingers, gently tease and pull apart the root-ball, dividing it into several substantially sized pieces. It may be necessary to cut through some roots, but never just slice through the soil-ball. Discard old pieces from the plant's centre and use only young, outer parts.

3 Select a clean pot, slightly smaller than before but large enough to accommodate the roots. Place compost in its base and position a divided piece in the centre. Hold the plant so that the soil-mark which indicates its earlier depth in a pot is about 12mm (½in) below the pot's rim. Then, gently trickle compost around the roots, spreading it evenly and in layers. Fill and firm compost to within 12mm (½in) of the rim, then lightly but thoroughly water it. Allow excess moisture to drain.

CANE CUTTINGS

These are created by cutting bare stems into pieces 7.5–13cm (3–5in) long and either inserting them vertically into pots of sandy compost or pressing them horizontally on the surface. Yuccas (*below*) and dumb canes (*right*) are increased in this way.

1 Specially prepared cuttings of yuccas are sometimes available. Their ends are usually covered with wax to prevent dehydration. Cut off a sliver from the lower end, but leave the top intact.

2 Select a small pot, about 7.5cm (3in) wide, and fill and firm the base with equal parts moist peat and sharp sand. Do not use a large pot as this may create a large amount of cold, wet compost around the cutting's base.

3 Insert the cutting, bare side downwards, about 5cm (2in) deep and trickle compost around it. Hold the cutting to ensure that it is kept upright, in the centre of the pot and with its base standing firmly on the compost.

4 Use your fingers to firm the compost evenly around the cutting. When finished, the compost's surface should be about 12mm (½in) below the pot's rim. Water, using a watering-can with a fine rose to water the compost. Do not use strong jets of water, as this may wash compost over the rim of the pot.

5 To encourage the cutting to root rapidly, place the pot and its cutting in an opaque plastic bag loosely tied at the neck. The plastic bag helps to retain humidity and warmth around the cutting and protects it from draughts.

Keep the bag in an accessible position and provide an even temperature with gentle warmth. Regularly inspect the compost (about every ten days) to ensure it does not become dry, and water lightly as before if necessary. When shoots appear, remove the bag and bring the pot into the light. Make sure that humidity is maintained and protect it from draughts. Slowly acclimatize the plant to room conditions.

HORIZONTAL CANE CUTTINGS

Dumb canes (*Dieffenbachia*) when aged often have several long, bare stems with small tufts of leaves at their top. Instead of discarding these plants, cut their stems into pieces about 7.5cm (3in) long. When forming cuttings from a dumb cane, either wear gloves or ensure that after touching the sap fingers are not put on eyes or into mouths. Wash your hands in soapy water, then rinse them.

1 Use a sharp knife to cut a thick, healthy stem from the congested base of a dumb cane. Cut low down to ensure that a short, unsightly stub does not remain on the plant, and take care not to damage the plant.

3 Fill a wide pot with equal parts moist peat and sharp sand and firm it to 12mm (½in) below the rim. Press each cutting to half its thickness into the compost and secure with pieces of bent wire.

2 Cut the stem into several pieces, each about 7.5cm (3in) long. Make sure that each length has at least one strong and healthy bud, as these will create good upward growth and develop into healthy new shoots.

4 Water the compost, allow to drain and place a plastic dome over the pot. Alternatively, insert small pieces of split cane around the pot's edge and draw a plastic bag over them. Use an elastic band to secure it around the pot.

PROBLEMS WITH HOUSEPLANTS

Unlike plants grown outdoors, houseplants are in artificial surroundings: their roots are confined in a small amount of compost that can be easily excessively watered or underwatered; they are frequently exposed to high temperatures even though the intensity of light is poor; and the temperature may fluctuate rapidly throughout the day and, in winter, be cold at night when heating systems are turned down or off. It is remarkable, therefore, that so many houseplants succeed and this is invariably due to the enthusiasm and vigilance of houseplant growers.

The pests and diseases most often seen on houseplants are featured on pages 36 and 37, while cultural problems are featured on page 35. Most houseplants underachieve and this is because they are not regularly fed. Those that are given a balanced diet have a better chance of surviving an infestation of pests or diseases than if undernourished and struggling for life. On the other hand, do not feed plants excessively, as this may make the compost toxic retarding growth or even killing them. Nor should you feed summer-flowering or foliage plants after late summer, as this encourages lush growth that is susceptible to pests and diseases, just when the plant is preparing to take a winter rest.

APPLYING CHEMICALS

There are several ways in which to apply chemicals to plants: spraying with a concentrated insecticide diluted in clean water is the most popular method. Some liquid sprays are ready to use. Dusting plants is also effective, but may leave an unattractive residue. Watering compost with a systemic insecticide and using insecticidal sticks are other methods.

Inserting an insecticidal stick into compost is a quick, clean and effective way to control pests in houseplants. Each stick contains a systemic insecticide which makes a plant toxic to insects.

Dusting plants with a powder is not a popular way to apply insecticides to houseplants, but it is quick and effective; when using powder, ensure that you distribute it evenly, and take the plant outdoors to avoid inhaling it and to protect furniture and drapes.

When applying a liquid spray, first put the plant inside a clean dustbin or large plastic bag. Then, apply the spray and leave the container closed for an hour. Remove the plant and allow fumes to disperse before replacing it indoors.

CULTURAL PROBLEMS

In addition to being damaged by pests and diseases (*see pages 36 and 37*), plants can become unhealthy through incorrect conditions, such as too little or too much water, excessive shade or strong sunlight, inappropriate temperatures, excessive humidity or insufficient food.

Some of the cultural problems are detailed here.

Variegated leaves become green if the plant is not in good light. Re-position the plant near a window.

Flowers become dry and rapidly fade if compost becomes dry, the temperature is too high, the air too dry or if the plant is in dense shade.

Leaves curl at their edges, then fall off, if the plant is in a cold draught, the temperature is low or the compost has been excessively watered.

Lower leaves become dry and crisp, and eventually fall off, through the compost being too dry, temperatures excessively high, or because there is too little light.

A white, powdery coating on a clay pot usually indicates that the plant has been excessively fed. It also means that the water may contain a great deal of chalk.

Leaves sometimes develop holes in their centre or along the outer edge. This is because they either have been knocked by people or pets, or are infested with pests such as caterpillars (see page 37).

Flower buds fall off if the compost or air is dry, the plant is in poor light or, in the case of some cacti, if the plant is moved and knocked.

Leaves wilt if compost is either very wet or dry. Excessively dry air and too much heat also causes wilting. During hot days, plants may temporarily wilt in early afternoon, but recover by evening.

Leaves wilt and decay if the compost is too wet. This especially applies to foliage plants during winter.

Blemishes occur on leaves through a number of causes: burnt areas appear after leaves with water droplets on their surfaces are left in strong sunlight. Diseases such as leaf spot (see page 36) also produce holes.

Green slime appears on clay pots if the compost has been excessively watered. The slime may also appear on the surface of compost.

PESTS AND DISEASES

Pests and diseases soon devastate houseplants if they remain undetected or neglected. Leaves, stems, shoots and flowers can all be affected, as well as roots. Prevention is easier than trying to eliminate an established colony of pests or a severe infection of a disease. Buying only clean and healthy plants reduces the risk of most pests or diseases infecting your plants. If you are doubtful about the health of a plant, isolate it for a couple of weeks before introducing it into a room full of other plants.

When watering plants, cleaning leaves or removing dead flowers, thoroughly inspect plants to ensure they are clean and healthy. If a problem is noticed, treat them immediately, before other plants become affected. Use only clean potting composts and never take cuttings from infected plants.

HOUSEPLANT DISEASES

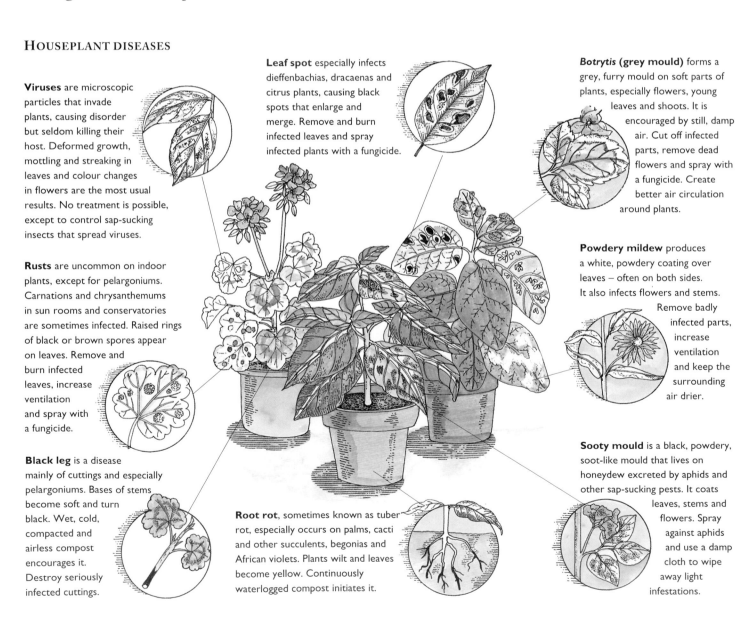

Viruses are microscopic particles that invade plants, causing disorder but seldom killing their host. Deformed growth, mottling and streaking in leaves and colour changes in flowers are the most usual results. No treatment is possible, except to control sap-sucking insects that spread viruses.

Rusts are uncommon on indoor plants, except for pelargoniums. Carnations and chrysanthemums in sun rooms and conservatories are sometimes infected. Raised rings of black or brown spores appear on leaves. Remove and burn infected leaves, increase ventilation and spray with a fungicide.

Black leg is a disease mainly of cuttings and especially pelargoniums. Bases of stems become soft and turn black. Wet, cold, compacted and airless compost encourages it. Destroy seriously infected cuttings.

Leaf spot especially infects dieffenbachias, dracaenas and citrus plants, causing black spots that enlarge and merge. Remove and burn infected leaves and spray infected plants with a fungicide.

Root rot, sometimes known as tuber rot, especially occurs on palms, cacti and other succulents, begonias and African violets. Plants wilt and leaves become yellow. Continuously waterlogged compost initiates it.

Botrytis **(grey mould)** forms a grey, furry mould on soft parts of plants, especially flowers, young leaves and shoots. It is encouraged by still, damp air. Cut off infected parts, remove dead flowers and spray with a fungicide. Create better air circulation around plants.

Powdery mildew produces a white, powdery coating over leaves – often on both sides. It also infects flowers and stems. Remove badly infected parts, increase ventilation and keep the surrounding air drier.

Sooty mould is a black, powdery, soot-like mould that lives on honeydew excreted by aphids and other sap-sucking pests. It coats leaves, stems and flowers. Spray against aphids and use a damp cloth to wipe away light infestations.

HOUSEPLANT PESTS

Vigilance is essential to prevent a small houseplant infestation becoming an epidemic and damaging a large number of plants. As well as inspecting plants, make sure that pots are checked too.

Always inspect newly bought plants as well as those given to you by friends; however well-meaning, they may introduce pests to your clean plants. And never use dirty potting compost as it may harbour pests and diseases.

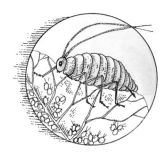

Aphids are soft-bodied, usually green and suck sap from leaves and petals, causing mottling and distortion. Also, they excrete honeydew which attracts sooty mould. Spray plants regularly, especially in summer.

Caterpillars are seldom seen indoors, but occasionally in sun rooms and conservatories. They chew holes in leaves. Pick off and destroy them and spray with an insecticide. Repeat the spray, as necessary.

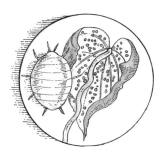

Cyclamen mites are minute, spider-like pests that infest plants such as cyclamen, African violets and pelargoniums. They cause stunting, leaves curl and become wrinkled and flowers distort and fall off. Burn infested plants.

Earwigs attack outdoor as well as indoor plants. They are rarely seen during daytime but at night they chew leaves and flowers, causing ragged holes and edges. Check for them at night – they hide under leaves and flowers – pick off and destroy them.

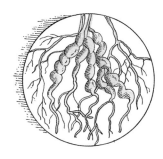

Eelworms are microscopic worms. There are several different types, including some that infest chrysanthemums or bulbs and some that cause irregular, corky swellings on roots (root-knot eelworm). If these worms are seen on the plant, it must be burned.

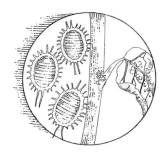

Mealy bugs resemble small woodlice covered in white, woolly wax. They cluster on the stems and under leaves of subtropical and tropical plants, sucking sap and causing leaves to yellow. Wipe off with cotton buds dipped in methylated spirits or alcohol.

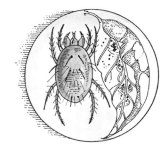

Red spider mites are minute, spider-like pests which infest the undersides of leaves and suck sap, causing speckling and yellow blotches. Daily mist-spraying of leaves helps to prevent an attack. Also, use a systemic insecticide. Burn seriously infected plants.

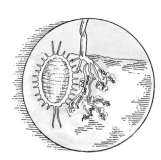

Root mealy bugs resemble small woodlice and live on the outer roots of plants in pots. They chew roots, especially of cacti and other succulents. Plants wilt and deteriorate. Inspect roots, especially when plants are repotted. Drench the compost in an insecticide.

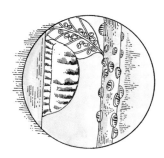

Scale insects are first apparent when plants become sticky. Swollen, protective, waxy-brown discs appear and female scale insects produce their young under them. Wipe off with cotton buds dipped in methylated spirits or alcohol. Burn seriously infected plants.

Thrips are tiny, dark brown, fly-like pests with light-coloured legs and wings. They jump from plant to plant, sucking leaves and flowers, causing silvery streaks and mottling. Flowers become distorted. Plants with dry compost suffer most. Spray several times with insecticides.

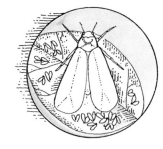

Whitefly are small, white and moth-like and when disturbed flutter around their host plant. Their young are green, suck sap and excrete honeydew, encouraging the presence of sooty mould. Eradication is not easy; spray repeatedly with insecticides.

FLOWERING PLANTS

Flowering plants bring life and colour to a room. The choice of plants can help to express the mood and decorative style, and their colours can highlight the room's colour scheme or add a pleasing counterpoint. Strongly perfumed flowers, such as jasmine will scent a whole room, while others, such as fairy primrose, give off a subtle fragrance that adds to the atmosphere almost indefinably.

Many indoor plants (pelargoniums and wax begonias, for example) flower almost non-stop, while others have a short but wonderful burst of flower. Plants such as the bromeliads have such good qualities of leaf and shape that their flowers are merely a bonus. Some will flourish indoors for years on end when cared for properly, while others are normally thrown out after flowering – although some of these can be made to flower again if you can find somewhere suitable to keep them during their resting period.

You can have plants in flower indoors all year round. Impulse buyers can find something to their liking in any season in shops and garden centres, but with a little planning you can also produce your own flowering plants for very little cost and enjoy the pleasure of growing them for yourself.

SIMPLE OR EXOTIC

You can create very different effects with indoor flowering plants, depending on your choice. Plants which can also be grown outside, such as pansies, busy Lizzies, chrysanthemums, primroses, pelargoniums, and many of the spring-flowering bulbs can have the effect of bringing the garden into the room when grown indoors, and often also of changing the seasons. The more tender plants, which do not grow outdoors in temperate climates, such as African violets, amaryllis, hibiscus and stephanotis, often flourish for many years, adding a more exotic touch, which increases in its impact with their size. If you have a conservatory which is heated in winter you can indulge in a taste for tropical plants of a most dramatic kind.

ABOVE A summer-flowering plant such as allamanda (*Allamanda cathartica* 'Grandiflora') earns its keep in all seasons. Its well-shaped leaves are evergreen and the plant can be trimmed to forma bush or trained as a sun room climber.
OPPOSITE A cool and calming atmosphere is created by a mixed display of flowering plants in which azaleas (*Rhododendron* species) dominate.

GROWING HEALTHY PLANTS

For a very short-term effect a flowering plant can be used in almost any situation. But if the plant is to thrive it must be given the same sort of conditions as those it (or the plants from which it has been developed) enjoys in the wild. Most plants that flower need good light, but many positively dislike the strong light of a window in full sun and there are many candidates for situations with indirect light. For good flowering from plants in pots, you also need to feed them regularly, and, to encourage continued flowering, or flowering over a long period, to remove the flowers as they die. As with all plants, the correct compost type is important when you pot up your own plants or repot bought ones.

DISPLAYING FLOWERING PLANTS

Flowering plants lend themselves to every form of display and they can be displayed in anything from hanging bowls and baskets to an indoor window box. They can be grouped in containers, with or without green plants, or shown off with 'still-life' objects. One striking plant in a handsome pot makes a focal point on a windowsill or low table and a single flowering plant, which can be changed with the seasons, is also an excellent means of enlivening a group of foliage plants.

Giving some thought to the container is often the way to make plants have the most impact. For a plant standing on its own, or for groups of single plants, each in its own pot, the choice of container or cache pot is vital. It must be in proportion with the plant, and it must suit the style of the room. All sorts of containers can be used as pots or pot holders. Choose baskets, old pottery or china, chamber pots and kitchenware for a simple 'country' look; plain, well-designed china, earthenware, plastic or metal containers, and basketware in simple shapes for a more sophisticated alternative.

GROUPING IN POTS

A beautiful azalea or camellia is often best standing alone in a complementary pot where it can be admired to the full. But less showy flowering plants group well with other plants.

With plants grown in individual pots, you can regroup plants easily.

1 Group plants in their own pots for a versatile display. To avoid damaging plants by moving them in and out of the container, plan first on a ring of cardboard the same size as the container, where you can move them around safely.

2 The tallest plants should go towards the middle and the lowest round the edges. Trailing plants will soften the edges of the container and soon hide the gaps between the pots. Usually one tall plant at the centre of the arrangement is best. Keep short-lived flowering pot plants near to the edge, so that you can move them later. A layer of small pebbles or clay pellets at the base of the container will absorb excess water from the pots and help to provide humidity.

A pink and red kalanchoe (*Kalanchoe blossfeldiana*) add warmth and colour to a collection of foliage plants. The plants used here are variegated ivies (*Hedera helix*), creeping fig (*Ficus pumila*) and young variegated ficus (*Ficus benjamina* 'Variegata').

PLANTING IN GROUPS

Planting in the same compost within a container needs to be planned bearing in mind the plants' varying growth rates and flowering periods. Plants in the same container must also have the same soil and watering requirements. All plants for grouping (even if they remain in separate pots) must share lighting and temperature needs.

A pot plant azalea (*Rhododendron simsii* and *R. obtusum* hybrids) draws the eye and can form a centrepiece for a table or windowsill, standing on its own. But if there is enough space and light, a group of azaleas, or azaleas mixed with other plants, can be breathtaking, (see pages 38 and 42).

3 Fill the container almost to the top with potting compost to which you have added charcoal to keep it sweet. For a hanging bowl or basket a lightweight peat- or fibre-based compost is best. Unless the container has a firm base, balance it in a bucket, as shown below.

1 To plan the design of a group for planting in a container, arrange the plants in their pots on a piece of cardboard the same shape and size as the container, as before.

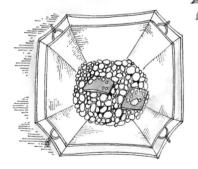

2 When you are satisfied with the arrangement from all angles, prepare the container for planting.

Begin by placing a generous layer of gravel or small pebbles in the base of the container to ensure good drainage. If there are large holes, cover each with a piece of broken pot first.

4 Remove the plants from their pots (which should have been well watered a few hours beforehand) one by one, and begin to plant from the centre. Add more compost as you go, tucking each plant well in. Leave a gap of about 5cm (2in) for watering below the container rim.

UNUSUAL CONTAINERS

More or less anything which has sides and a base can be used as a planting pot or an ornamental container for plants in their own pots. Old tea caddies, storage jars and junk-shop finds, teapots and salad bowls, and even wooden boxes can give an original look to a plant display. Plastic containers can be painted in a plain colour and dappled with second and third colours, simple containers can be covered in hessian or printed paper, and baskets can be spray-painted. Blocks of wood can be placed inside a container to raise the height of the plant. Containers in metal and anything that is not waterproof are best used to hold pots, rather than for direct planting. Place a large plastic box inside, or line with layers of plastic topped with newspaper to absorb excess water draining from the flower pots.

Planting directly into containers not designed for plants demands some thought because of the lack of drainage. The base of the container must be lined with a good layer of clay pellets which absorb moisture and give good, natural drainage. Charcoal mixed with the potting medium will help to keep it sweet.

FLOWERING HOUSEPLANTS

A well-cared for plant that has 'lived' in the house for several years and that still flowers duly in its season is as much a source of pleasure – and pride – as a well-polished antique. These are the houseplants, as opposed to pot plants that come and go and are often dispensed with at the end of the flowering season. Many flowering houseplants can become quite large and will eventually need to be given plenty of room, perhaps in a hall with a high ceiling or standing by a patio door, or even in a conservatory or sun room. But there is still plenty of choice for those who cannot provide space for very large plants.

To stand the test of time, a plant must be well chosen in the first place. There is no point in being seduced by a light-craving, hot-house plant if you live in a dark cottage, and if your fifth-floor flat gets the full glare of the midday sun a shade-lover is not for you. Choose from the justly popular, well-established favourites that are widely available, or search out something a little different from a specialist grower.

HEALTHY PLANTS

Buy from a reputable supplier, and choose a healthy looking specimen that is not pot-bound and that has plenty of new buds, and vigorous, not soft, growth. Your plant will need to be repotted, into a pot one size larger, as its roots fill its pot. This is done at the end of the dormant period and may be an annual job, especially while the plant is young and growing quickly. Once the plant has exhausted the minerals in the compost (in about 6–8 weeks), feed it with proprietary fertilizer during the growing period. The plants described below are some of the best to consider.

Acalypha hispida (**chenille plant**) An old favourite that is grown for its softly drooping tassels, which hang from the stems from mid-summer to mid-autumn. These are made up of hundreds of minuscule flowers – usually in deep scarlet, though there are varieties with cream and greenish tassels. The plant grows to a manageable size of 90cm–1.2m (33–44in), spread 30–45cm (11–14in).

Light: Bright, indirect light.

Flamingo flower (*Anthurium scherzerianum*) has bold foliage as well as striking red flowers in spring and summer.

LEFT Azaleas and pot chrysanthemums mingle with orchids in this cool conservatory. A mixture of complementary containers and surfaces at different heights helps to enrich the display.

Temperature: Normal room temperature in summer, not less than 15°C (59°F) in winter. Water freely in summer; keep compost moist in winter. Feed every 10–14 days from spring to autumn.

Aeschynanthus lobbianus (summer-flowering lipstick vine) With its trailing cascades of little fleshy leaves and tubular red flowers with cream throats, it is ideal for hanging baskets in sun rooms and conservatories.

Stems are 45–60cm (18–24in) long.

Light: Very bright light (but avoid full sun in summer).

Temperature: Very warm in summer, cooler in winter, with minimum of 13°C (55°F).

Water with tepid water, freely in summer, sparingly in winter. Feed monthly during late spring and throughout the summer. Keep surrounding air humid by mist-spraying.

Anthurium scherzerianum (flamingo flower or pigtail plant) Each intriguing red, palette-shaped spathe, has a curly, wick-like spire of tiny flowers, from spring to autumn. There is also a white variety. It is a compact 30cm (12in) high and 30–38cm (12–15in) across and has attractive, lance-shaped leaves.

Similar, but larger – up to 45cm (18in) high and 30cm (12in) across – is *A. andreanum*, the oilcloth flower or painter's palette, which has a straight 'tail' and is available in pink and orange.

Light: Bright, indirect light.

Temperature: Normal room temperatures in summer, 15–18°C (59–64°F) in winter.

Water generously in summer; keep the compost just moist in winter. Keep the surrounding air moist and feed every 10–14 days from mid-spring to early autumn.

ABOVE The lipstick or basket vines make excellent trailing plants for hanging baskets in a sun room or glazed porch. There are several species, but *Aeschynanthus lobbianus* is the most widely available. Deep-red flowers emerge from the purple-brown, hood-like outer cases.

LEFT When a fireplace is not in use it can be enlivened by a group of houseplants. These foliage plants are arranged informally to make an exuberant mix of plant forms with contrasting leaf shapes and patterns. Pot plants, cut flowers and ornaments complete the effect.

Aphelandra squarrosa **'Louisae' (Zebra plant)** Grown for its boldly patterned foliage as well as the pineapple-like yellow bracts which form the showy part of its flower heads. In this variety these are streaked with red and the plant will grow to be 75cm (30in) high and to about 40cm (16in) wide.

Light: Bright, indirect light.

Temperature: Normal room temperatures in summer; 12–15°C (54–59°F) in winter.

Water generously in summer and moderately in winter. Feed every 10–14 days. Cut off flower heads when they die, and cut the plant back to keep it bushy if necessary.

Begonia haageana **(elephant ear begonia)** Large, curiously shaped leaves make this plant interesting all year, and the pale-pink summer flowers are a bonus. *B. metallica*, the metallic leaf begonia, is known as a foliage plant, but it too has pretty flowers borne in white clusters in late summer. *B. haageana* will grow 1.2m (4ft) high with a spread of 60cm (2ft) and *B. metallica* measures about 90cm (3ft) high and 60cm (2ft) across.

Light: Bright, indirect light, with some direct sun in winter.

Temperature: Normal room temperatures in summer; constant 13–15.5°C (55–60°F) in winter. Too much summer heat can be fatal.

Keep the atmosphere very humid, especially in summer. Water moderately in summer, sparingly in winter. Feed every 14 days in summer.

Beloperone guttata **(shrimp plant)** Now officially known as *Justicia brandegeana,* this plant is a charming curiosity, its flower heads made up of shrimp-like bracts terminating in a tubular, white flower. It makes a small bush 30–40cm (12–16in) high and across and is easy to grow, provided you are able to give it a sunny windowsill.

Light: Bright sunlight, but with protection from full summer sun.

Temperature: Normal, warm room temperatures in summer; a cooler 10–16°C (50–61°F) in winter, with a minimum of 7°C (45°F).

Zebra plant (*Aphelandra squarrosa*) will lose its magnificent leaves very quickly if its roots become dry. It shuns cold, draughts and bright sun and should be regularly fed, and watered generously during summer and autumn, using slightly warm, lime-free water. The variety 'Louisae' is generally considered to be the best to grow as a houseplant.

ABOVE The pinky-white flowers of the shrimp plant (*Beloperone guttata*) project from overlapping bracts in brownish pink and really do look very shrimp like. Grown on a sunny windowsill the plant is covered with flowers from spring to autumn.

ABOVE Elephant's ear begonia (*Begonia haageana*) is one of the less common begonias. Its large leaves make it an unusual looking plant, but it is fairly undemanding.

Water generously in summer, sparingly in winter. Grow two or three plants together for a good show; cut them back in spring if they begin to get 'leggy'.

Bougainvillea glabra A young bougainvillea is a wonderful showy plant for a sunny windowsill. But it is a scrambler that will need to be trained and given ample space as it grows. The papery, purple 'flowers' are really bracts and grow in clusters throughout the summer.

Light: Must have ample bright light all year round.

Temperature: Hot in summer, cooler 7–12°C (45–54°F) in winter.

Water sparingly in summer and keep the compost almost dry in winter. The plant grows best in a conservatory when more than three years old.

Brunfelsia calycina (**yesterday, today and tomorrow**) A shrubby plant whose pretty flowers change colour from violet to white as they age. It flowers all summer when growing well, and grows to 60cm (2ft) high and 30cm (12in) across.

Light: Bright, indirect light.

Temperature: Warm in summer, but not above 21°C (70°F); constant 10–13°C (50–55°F) in winter.

Water generously, mist-spray the leaves, and feed once a month when in flower; water sparingly when resting.

Campanula isophylla (**Italian bellflower** or **trailing campanula**) This is a low-growing, 15cm (6in) high plant with a spread of 30–45cm (12–18in), available in blue or white. It flowers beautifully all summer long, and with its trailing habit is ideal for a tall pot or stand, or a hanging basket.

Light: Good, indirect light.

Temperature: Warm, but not too hot, in summer 15–19°C (59–66°F); cooler 4–10°C (39–50°F) in winter.

Keep the compost moist and feed every week to 10 days in summer. Cut back all the stems after flowering and let the plant rest, watering very sparingly, in winter.

Several calatheas are grown as houseplants, as much for their large, attractive leaves as for their flowers. *Calathea crocata* has flowers like small orchids.

ABOVE Bougainvillea or paper flower, a native of Brazil, grows rampantly outdoors in Mediterranean countries. In cooler areas it makes a spectacular deciduous indoor climber for a warm, light, sunny position. Several varieties and species are available, including *B. glabra* shown here.

ABOVE Elatior or hiemnalis begonias flower best in autumn and winter. The flowers are full and beautiful and come in a range of mainly yellow, orange and pink shades, often flushed with subtly contrasting colours.

***Cestrum nocturnum* (night jessamine)** Similar to jasmine, with an equally strong and beautiful scent. When young this night-flowering plant is ideal for a light living room, but it can grow to 3m (10ft) and then needs a conservatory or large, light space.

Light: Very bright light, but with protection from full summer sun.

Temperature: Normal room temperature in summer; not less than 7°C (45°F) in winter.

Water generously in summer and moderately in winter. Train the twining stems up canes and along wires.

***Columnea* (goldfish plant)** There are several popular columneas and all are trailing plants for sun rooms and conservatories, and are particularly useful as they flower throughout the winter, from autumn to early spring.

Columnea microphylla Trails to a length of up to 1.8m (6ft) and has bright orange-red flowers and hairy leaves; the flowers of *C. × banksii* are similar but with orange markings, the stems a more modest 90cm (3ft) and the leaves dark and glossy; *C. gloriosa* has stems of up to 1.2m (4ft) bearing scarlet flowers with a yellow patch and its pale-green leaves are hairy. The species *C. gloriosa* has produced a variety with purple leaves, 'Purpurea'.

Light: Bright light, but not direct sun.

Temperature: About 16°C (61°F) in winter, with a minimum of 13°C (55°F); normal in summer.

These plants need very humid conditions and the compost must be kept moist at all times. Feed weekly as soon as flower buds appear.

ABOVE *Columnea hirta* is one of the smaller columneas. Its strong, creeping stems produce a mass of red flowers in spring.

LEFT A sun room provides the space, and growing conditions, for vigorous climbing plants, which can be trained up netting or trellis and along wires (fixed in place before the plants are introduced). Parasol plant (*Schefflera arboricola*) dominates the main wall, and the tall, large-leaved greenhouse border plant known as house lime or indoor linden (*Sparmannia africana*) towers in front of it. The fast-growing, fronded silky oak (*Grevillea robusta*) in brighter light by the window forms a leafy background for tall border chrysanthemums and the two white azaleas standing in a cool position on the stone floor.

Cuphea ignea (**cigar flower**)
A compact shrub that produces its long, tubular, bright-red flowers, which are tipped dark purple and ash white, from spring until the beginning of winter, or even longer. *C .i.* 'Alba' has white flowers and *C. i.* 'Variegata' has yellow-marked leaves.

Light: Very bright light, but with some shade from full sun in summer.

Temperature: Normal summer temperatures, and a cooler 10–13°C (50–55°F) winter rest. Cigar plant enjoys a spell outside in warm summer weather as long as good humidity is maintained.

Water generously during spring and summer and feed every two weeks. Water sparingly during the winter and do not feed.

Dipladenia sanderi 'Rosea' (syn. *Mandevilla sanderi* 'Rosea' and sometimes knows as mandevilla) This is a gorgeous and versatile plant. Its large pink flowers appear in profusion throughout the summer if the air is kept warm and humid, and it can be trained as a climber, up to 4.5m (15ft) or pruned as a shrub. A white-flowering species, *D. laxa*, which is highly fragrant, is available.

Light: Give good light, but protect from strong sun.

Temperature: Try to maintain a steady 21°C (70°F) in summer and 15.5°C (60°F) in winter, with a minimum of 13°C (55°F).

Water generously in summer and fairly sparingly in winter; feed the plant weekly while it is in flower.

Episcia A close relation of African violets, *Episcias* are flowering houseplants grown also for their foliage. *E. cupreata*, the flame violet or carpet plant, has flame-red flowers and quilted leaves, and *E. dianthiflora*, the lace flower, has plump, downy leaves and white flowers with fringed petals which resemble those of garden pinks. Both grow only 7.5cm (3in) high, with trailing stems or runners, up to 30cm (12in) long, from which new plants can be grown.

Light: Good light, but avoiding strong sun.

ABOVE The quilted leaves of flame violet (*Episcia cupreata*) have bronze-tinted highlights. Almost hidden among the leaves are pretty, little, red flowers with bright-yellow eyes which are shaped like flaring tubes.

Temperature: Normal room temperatures, with a winter minimum of 13°C (55°F). Try to give these plants a slight drop in temperature each evening and ensure that the air around them is humid by mist-spraying and standing their pots in a dish of wet pebbles.

Crown of thorns (*Euphorbia milii*) is attractive for its rounded leaves and thorny stems, which grow woody as the plant ages. But the waxy bracts surrounding its tiny yellow flowers can make a wonderful show if the plant is given warmth and good light. It is well worth hunting out the unusual white-flowering form.

PERFUMED FLOWERING PLANTS

Many flowering plants are fragrant, including some not generally known for their scent, such as some cyclamen, daffodils and the houseplant primroses. Conversely, some plants known for their scent come in unscented forms too. It is always best to be guided by one's nose.

Heavily scented plants, such as hyacinths, hoyas, jasmine and stephanotis, need to be carefully positioned. While most people like a gentle fragrance in a bedroom some find these strong perfumes overpowering. Equally, scented plants can be incompatible with food and are not ideal for a small kitchen or dining room, while plants such as night jessamine (*Cestrum nocturnum*) give out more fragrance at night and are perfect for a sitting room. Scented plants placed in the hall perfume the whole house and add an extra welcome.

Euphorbia milii (**crown of thorns**) This handsome plant, also known as *E. splendens*, is another plant which is grown for the colourful, showy bracts (in this case, red, yellow or white) which surround its tiny, insignificant flowers. It has rather sprawling stems with prominent spines and grows to a height of 90cm (3ft). It flowers during spring and early summer, and almost non-stop in a really bright light.

Light: Bright, but shaded from midday summer sun.

Temperature: Normal room temperatures, which do not fall below 13°C (55°F) in winter.

This popular plant is very undemanding as long as you can find a sunny spot for it.

Hibiscus rosa-sinensis (**hibiscus or rose of China**) This is another good plant for a sunny position. Most often seen in deep-reddish pink, it can also have yellow, orange, pale-pink or white flowers. The large flowers are short-lived, but new buds open regularly throughout the summer.

A well-cared for hibiscus can live for many years and grow to 1.5m (5ft) high if not cut back. The variety 'Cooperi' has cream and crimson variegated leaves.

Light: Good light.

Temperature: An even 18°C (64°F) or above all year round produces non-stop flowering; 10–15.5°C (50–60°F) in winter if you wish to give the plant a rest.

Water the plant fairly generously and feed once a week while it is in flower. Water only moderately and do not feed in winter if you going to allow the plant a dormant period.

Hoya carnosa (**wax plant**) This plant looks and smells exotic with its clusters of waxy, scented flowers but is not too difficult to grow. Its climbing stems will grow up to 4.5m (15ft) and must be trained up canes or trellis, or along wires.

Light: Very bright light, with some shade from strong summer sun.

Temperature: Summer minimum 16°C (61°F); winter around 10°C (50°F) and not below 7°C (45°F).

Give the plant fresh air in summer, but keep the humidity high. It looks natural and attractive trained up a moss pole.

Another popular hoya, *H. Bella* or miniature wax plant grows lower and bushier, and is perfect for a hanging basket. This species needs more warmth in winter 13°C (55°F) and must be well protected from strong summer sun.

Ixora coccinea (**flame of the woods**) This eye-catching plant needs some care. Its big flower heads are clustered with little red flowers (white, yellow and pink in some varieties) and it forms an evergreen bushy plant that can grow up to 38cm (15in) in a year.

Light: Give bright filtered light, away from direct sun.

ABOVE The orange-flowering varieties of hibiscus or rose of China (*Hibiscus rosa-sinensis*) include 'Tivoli' (above) and 'Royal Orange' which is illustrated below.

Hibiscus or rose of China (*Hibiscus rosa-sinensis*) is a long-lived plant native to China, which is all too often lost through poor treatment when grown as a houseplant. Underwatering causes buds to drop and leaves to fall and underfeeding reduces flowering; low humidity, draughts or sudden temperature changes, as well as over-generous watering, are also damaging.

Temperature: Provide a warm 21–22°C (70–72°F) in summer and minimum of 15.5°C (60°F) in winter.

Water and mist spray regularly, using tepid, boiled water, but water only sparingly and rest the plant for about two months after flowering. Do not repot unless absolutely necessary. Use an ericaceous, acid compost.

***Jasminum polyanthum* (pink jasmine)** The lovely pink jasmine, with its pink buds and clusters of white, scented flowers, is fairly easy to grow and flowers indoors in winter. A climber that can reach 3m (10ft), it is generally restricted and trained over a hoop.

Light: Bright light.

Temperature: Does best in cooler rooms heated to 7–10°C (45–50°F) in winter.

Train the plant by wrapping its tendrils round the support, and cut it back after flowering.

***Manettia inflata* (climbing firecracker plant** or **firecracker vine)** An undemanding and attractive plant. It grows well in normal room conditions, and flowers almost all year round. Long, red, downy tubular flowers, tipped with yellow, peep out from glossy, deep-green leaves. Stems grow rapidly and can reach 3m (10ft).

Light: Full sun.

Temperature: Winter minimum: 15.5°C (50°F).

Keep the compost moist at all times, and water more generously in spring and summer. Train the plant up a pyramid of canes, tying in the new shoots as they grow.

With their waxy flowers and leaves, hoyas or wax plants look almost unreal. They bear beautiful, starry, headily scented flowers with deep rose-red or purple centres. *Hoya bella*, shown, is larger and more trailing than the more compact and bushier *Hoya carnosa*.

The pink jasmine (*Jasminum polyanthum*) is only half-hardy in temperate areas and therefore mainly grown as a houseplant, when it flowers from mid-winter to spring. Outdoors and in sheltered areas it flowers during late spring and early summer. The common white jasmine (*J. officinale*) is hardier and widely grown outdoors in temperate climates.

Pachystachys lutea (lollipop plant or **golden shrimp plant)** A bright and fairly adaptable plant about 50cm (20in) high. It has bold, clear, yellow flower heads made up of overlapping bracts with little, white projecting flowers from spring to autumn.

Light: Good bright light, but not full sun.

Temperature: Normal room temperatures throughout the year, with a winter minimum of 13°C (55°F).

Water generously when the plant is in flower, but quite sparingly in winter. Keep the surrounding air moist when warm. Repot and trim back every spring.

Passiflora caerulea (**common passion flower**) Also known as blue passion flower and passion vine, its large and complex summer flowers can be followed by orange fruits.

Light: Bright sunlight.

Temperature: Normal summer temperatures. The plant must rest at about 10°C (50°F) in winter.

Water this plant extremely generously while it is in flower, but keep the compost just moist during winter. When young it can be trained round a hoop, but it is vigorous and does justice to a trellis as it grows. Too much feeding can encourage the plant to produce more leaves than flowers.

Pelargonium (**geranium**) An old favourite, at home in cottage and castle. There are three main types grown for their flowers: zonal or common, often with bold zones of contrasting colour on the leaves; regal, with bigger, fancier flowers and irregularly edged leaves; and ivy-leaved or trailing. If you make sure they have plenty of sun and are kept reasonably warm in winter, they will flower cheerfully all year round, but they can be given a cooler winter rest. The bushy types can be quite compact or can reach 60cm (24in) high with a spread of 25–45cm (10–18in).

Pelargonium peltatum (**Trailing geraniums**) These have shiny, ivy-like leaves and are perfect for hanging baskets or as part of a display on a light, open landing or indoor balcony. They trail for up to 90cm (3ft).

Light: Full sun (especially zonal and regal types).

Temperature: Normal room temperature year round, with a

ABOVE **The passion flower (*Passiflora caerulea*) can be grown outside even in temperate regions; it is also superb as a houseplant and bears intricately formed white and blue flowers from mid- to late summer. It needs support and when grown in a pot its stems can be twined around a large hoop of pliable canes or wire.**

The bright-yellow flower heads of the lollipop plant (*Pachystachys lutea*) are formed by a cone of overlapping bracts. It flowers from late spring to early autumn, and grows well in a room that is cool in summer.

winter minimum of 7–10°C (45–50°F).

Water fairly generously and feed every two weeks when in flower; if resting in lower temperatures keep the compost barely moist. Bushy types will become 'leggy' in inadequate light.

***Plumbago capensis* (cape leadwort)** This unattractively named plant has the most attractive blue flowers. It can be allowed to trail, but is best trained to a support. Like the passion flower it is fairly tolerant, but must have a cool winter rest.

Light: Fairly bright light but not full midday sun.

Temperature: Normal summer temperatures; 7-10°C (45–50°F) in winter.

Water generously when in flower in summer and autumn, sparingly in winter.

RIGHT *Pelargonium* 'Parasol' is typical of the regal type with its many-petalled flowers splashed in pink and white and streaked with deep-red markings.

'Pink Cascade' is typical of the trailing geraniums (*Pelargonium peltatum* varieties) with its bushy, trailing growth, ivy-like leaves, colourful flowers and delicate buds. These are perfect plants for a summer hanging basket in a porch or airy sun room.

RIGHT When young, cape leadwort (*Plumbago capensis*) is often trained round a hoop and grown on a windowsill, where its beautiful, phlox-like flowers can be admired throughout summer and into autumn. The plant is vigorous and stems can reach 1.20m (4ft) in length but can be trimmed in spring to keep them shorter.

***Saintpaulia* (African violet)**
Now one of the most familiar
of houseplants, thanks partly to
central heating and partly to
the ease with which new plants
can be propagated from the
velvety leaves. These pretty
little plants can be kept in
flower all year but they can be
quite fussy. Normal height is
7.5–10cm (3–4in), and spread
is 15–23cm (6–9in), but tiny,
and exquisite, miniature forms
are now becoming popular.

Light: Good, bright light,
avoiding strong sun.

Temperature: Steady
warmth year round; minimum
15.5°C (60°F).

African violets look well in
groups, and this helps keep
the humidity high, which is
essential, as is acid compost
and regular feeding.

***Spathiphyllum wallisii* (peace
lily)** An elegant plant with
long, gleaming leaves and tall
flowers consisting of a white,
sail-like spathe surrounding a
creamy-white flower spike.
The plant flowers from late
spring and through the whole
summer. It needs warmth and

ABOVE The flowers of the peace lily
(*Spathiphyllum wallisii*) are typical arum
lily flowers, unfurling into a spathe
(the white 'sail') and spadix (the central
flowering 'spike') and appearing
throughout summer. The hybrid
S. x 'Mauna Loa' flowers intermittently
throughout the year.

LEFT With its dark leaves and chaste
appearance, the peace lily is an ideal
plant for a white pot. It is grouped here
with two young silver net leaf plants
(*Fittonia verschaffeltii* 'Argyroneura').

African violets (*Saintpaulia*) need
to be grown in bright light and
where their dainty flowers can be
seen in close-up. Dead or
damaged leaves should be cut off
as soon as they appear, and plants
watered from the base to keep
the leaves dry.

humidity, summer shade and winter sun, and must not be subjected to draughts.

Light: Indirect light in summer; full light in winter.

Temperature: Winter minimum 10°C (50°F).

Feed every ten days throughout the year, but with the fertilizer diluted to half strength in winter.

Stephanotis floribunda Glossy, leathery leaves and headily scented, waxy flowers from early summer to mid-autumn make this plant desirable. Stephanotis will climb and spread to 3m (10ft) or so and needs to be trained to a trellis or along wires.

Light: Good light with shade from full sun in summer; full light in winter.

Temperature: Constant temperatures of about 18–21°C (64–70°F) in summer and 13°C (55°F) in winter.

During flowering, water generously and provide high humidity, especially when temperatures are high, and feed once every two weeks. Water sparingly in winter.

Streptocarpus × hybrida (cape primrose or cape cowslip) There is a wide choice of hybrids of the white-, pink-, mauve-, blue- or purple-flowered plant. This seems a misnomer, for the flowers resemble large violets or single foxgloves on long, upright stems. They grow from a loose rosette of rounded leaves.

Light: Good indirect light.

Temperature: Up to 15.5°C (60°F) in summer and a steady 10–13°C (50–55°F) in winter.

Water freely during the summer and stand the plant on a tray of wet pebbles. Water more sparingly in winter. Do not mist-spray and avoid wetting the leaves.

ABOVE Saintpaulias or African violets look lovely in groups. Their flowers have great intensity of colour and in some varieties the petals have a contrasting or frilled rim. The ruffs of large, downy leaves set off the flowers to perfection.

The exotically perfumed stephanotis thrives if kept in a fairly cool room in winter and protected at all times from draughts and sudden changes in temperature. The young plant looks pretty trained round a hoop.

ABOVE AND LEFT The flowers of cape primrose (*Streptocarpus x hybrida*) nod prettily from erect stems. If they are cut off as they die the plant will flower over a long period. The pale-throated flowers are often in shades of blue and lilac, and are usually patterned with dark veining towards the throat.

FLOWERING POT PLANTS

A pot plant will generally have less permanence than other indoor plants, either because it is difficult or impossible to keep it going once it has flowered, or because the plant is not a thing of beauty while it is 'resting' in preparation for its next flowering period. Pot plants make a colourful, and sometimes fragrant, contribution when in flower and are usually planted in the garden, or even thrown away, once the flowering period is over. Some are annuals, and so last only one season; others are very short-lived perennials, or perennials that have been reared in very special conditions, and sometimes also treated, so that they come into flower at an unusual time or retain what is in fact an unnatural dwarf habit. Many more pot plants have been developed and introduced commercially in recent years, and there is now a good choice available all year round.

SELECTING AND DISPLAYING

A healthy pot plant makes a good centre-piece for a table or windowsill, and a brightly coloured flowering plant placed in its pot among leaves and ferns brings the foliage to life. You may acquire your pot plant as a gift, but if you want to buy one, a visit to your garden centre at any time of year will give you a wide choice of pot plants in flower, and many supermarkets now have a good selection. There are also some lovely annuals, such as *Schizanthus* (butterfly flower), which can easily be grown from seed at home. Some of the best to buy, or grow from seed, are described here.

Achimines **hybrids (hot water plant)** Much grown by the Victorians, it has masses of slightly fragrant, bright pink, flaring trumpet flowers from spring to autumn. Mauve, red, white and blue varieties are also available. It is easily grown afresh each year from rhizomes (the underground stems).

Light: Bright light with shade from full sun.

Temperature: Normal room temperatures.

Water frequently with tepid water and feed weekly.

Pot chrysanthemums are now available throughout the year and they remain in flower for more than a month. When their display ends they are best discarded. They need bright light (but not full sun) in a fairly cool room. Keep the compost moist but not waterlogged.

Slipper flower (*Calcaeolaria* x *herbeohybrida*) is a biennial with distinctive puffed flowers which give it the alternative names pouch flower and pocketbook plant. Buy the plant when in bud and keep it in a cool, maximum 16°C (61°C), but bright and sunny position for late spring or early summer flowers which last a month or more.

Astilbe arendsii (**plume of feathers**) This garden plant makes a lovely indoor plant for spring and early summer. The plumes are usually in pink, but red and white varieties can be found.

Light: Fairly bright light with shade from full sun.

Temperature: Normal room temperatures.

Give the plant plenty of humidity and water it well. Plant it in a damp, semi-shaded part of the garden when it has finished flowering.

Begonia **species** The tuberous begonia hybrids, *B. × tuberhybrida*, with their beautiful, mainly double, rose-like flowers, make the most lovely flowering pot plants for the summer months.

Light: Bright, indirect light.

Temperatures: Normal summer room temperatures, with spring warmth to bring them into growth.

Keep the potting compost evenly moist.

Other good flowering begonias are *B. multiflora*, which has very similar, but slightly smaller, flowers and rather arching stems, making it good for hanging baskets, the justly popular *B. socotra* 'Gloire de Lorraine', with its masses of small pink flowers in winter, and the many elatior hybrids.

Erica Two forms of heather make excellent winter-flowering pot plants, *E. gracilis*, the cape heath, and *E. × hyemnalis*, but they must be kept in cool rooms and watered with soft water. Both have masses of tubular flowers, which are tiny, and pink or rosy-purple in *E. gracilis*, and larger, in pink with white tips in *E. × hyemnalis*.

Ericas need lime-free compost.
Light: Good light.
Temperature: 4.5–13°C (40–55°F).
Keep the potting compost constantly moist.

Exacum affine (**Arabian** or **Persian violet,** sometimes also known as **German violet**) This pretty plant has small, fragrant, mauve flowers with bright-yellow centres. It is compact, with heart-shaped leaves and it suits a coffee table or bedroom windowsill.

Light: Good bright light, but not strong sun.

Temperature: Normal room temperatures, with fresh air in hot weather.

Water generously and keep humidity high. Pinch out dying flowers and feed every ten days to have flowers throughout the summer.

ABOVE **The well-known** *Begonia elatior* hybrid begonias make popular pot plants as they produce a mass of flowers, single or double, and can be bought in flower all year round.

BELOW **Many colourful hybrids of the hot water plant or cupid's bower (***Achimenes* **hybrids) have been introduced in recent years, including those with variegated leaves. Given moisture-retentive compost and good light, all flower continually throughout the summer.**

Plume flower (*C. elosia plumosa,* sometimes sold as *C. argentea plumosa*) can be grown as a bedding plant, but its plumed flowers and bold, green leaves make a lovely summer display in a light airy room.

BELOW Hydrangeas create superb displays of colour from late spring to early summer. *Hydrangea macrophylla* (sometimes called hortensia) has large, round, flower heads up to 15–20cm (6–8in) wide. The petals can be white, blue, pink or red.

ABOVE Poinsettias (*Euphorbia pulcherrima*) have become a classic mid-winter plant. Their showy 'flowers' (which are really bracts) make a cheerful seasonal display. Most poinsettias have deep-crimson bracts, but white, pink and scarlet varieties are available.

Hydrangea macrophylla

Pot hydrangeas are available in flower from spring to autumn and can be planted out in the garden once they have flowered. The mop heads of flowers come in white and pastel shades which can be varied by using alkaline (for pink shades) or acid (for blue shades) compost. Hydrangeas do best in cool conditions.

Light: Good indirect light.
Temperature: Up to 20°C (68°F).

Water well when in flower, and feed once a week.

Primula malacoides (fairy primrose)

A dainty, short-lived plant that flowers during the winter and has a slight but lovely fragrance. It can be persuaded to flower for a second season if kept well. The primrose flowers, in a range of pinks and white, are carried in whorls on tall, straight stems, growing from rosettes of tooth-edged leaves.

Light: Bright, indirect light.
Temperature: A fairly cool 10–13°C (50–55°F).

Water generously and keep humidity high. Feed every two weeks.

Other winter-flowering primulas are *P. obconia*, the poison primrose, which has larger flowers and comes in a red variety as well as the pinks and pinky blues, and the Chinese primrose, *P. sinensis*, which has frilly-edged petals and comes in red and orange as well as muted bluey pinks. Beware of the poison primrose, which is indeed poisonous, and which can also cause allergic rashes in some people.

Flaming Katy (*Kalanchoe blossfeldiana*) can be bought in flower at any time. Red, orange, pink, yellow and white varieties are available. The plant can often be induced to flower again if it is trimmed back and given a rest in a cool, dim spot with reduced watering once the initial flowering is finished.

Senecio cruentus (**cineraria**) A well-known plant with daisy-like flowers in brightly coloured shades of blue to pink and red, each with a white centre. Despite being a popular gift plant, it is quite difficult to please. The compost must be kept moist, but must drain freely and the plant must not be exposed to draughts or high temperatures. Likes indirect light. Even room temperature, which must never be higher than 15°C (60°F).

The plants are usually available in late winter and spring, and flower for up to two months. Feed cinerarias once a fortnight to encourage new buds to form.

Sinningia speciosa (**gloxinia**) Increasingly exotic-looking hybrids of this plant have been bred in recent years. The rosettes of leaves are soft and velvety, and the large, flaring tubular, flowers often have contrast throats and may be bordered in white or contrasting colours.

Light: Bright, indirect light.
Temperature: A warm 20–22°C (68–72°F) day and night in summer (when the plant is in flower).

Keep the air humid by standing the plant pot on a tray of moist pebbles but do not spray the leaves or flowers, and water the plant from below. Feed gloxinias weekly.

ABOVE This gloxinia (*Sinningia* hybrid) has the characteristic brightly coloured and contrast-bordered petals and large velvety leaves.

LEFT Apart from the hardy primroses (*Primula acaulis*) there are several tender primula species grown indoors for winter flowers. Poison primrose (*P. obconica*) has the largest flowers and these have a lovely fragrance, but the leaves can provoke allergic reactions, especially if wet.

A healthy cineraria (*Senecio cruentus*) keeps its flowers longer if it is regularly fed and mist-sprayed. It should not be given too much heat.

POT PLANT TIPS

Many pot plants are seasonal, with solanums and poinsettias for Christmas (in the northern hemisphere); cyclamens and azaleas for winter or early spring; scented spring primroses, and plume flower (*Celosia*) and slipper flower (*Calceolaria*) for summer. But plants such as chrysanthemum and kalanchoe can be bought in flower all year.

Generous feeding and the removal of dying flowers should help to extend the flowering period, and most pot plants need good light; but check each plant's own care requirements carefully. Try to protect plants from sudden temperature changes and from draughts in winter, and remember that many winter flowers need temperatures that are a little lower than those of most living rooms.

BULBS

Many of the best-loved indoor flowering plants are grown from bulbs, or from the similar corms (which are technically stems) and tubers (underground storage organs). Most of all we associate bulbs with spring, and it is true that some of the long-time favourites are spring-flowering, with early indoor hyacinths, crocuses, daffodils and other forms of narcissi, and tulips reminding us that winter is on the way out. Today's specially prepared bulbs make spring narcissi and hyacinths available even for Christmas (in the Northern Hemisphere), a long time before they will be flowering in parks and gardens. But bulbs (and corms and tubers) can produce lovely flowers at all times of year.

It is usually best to consign all hardy bulbs that have been grown indoors to the garden after they have flowered as they cannot be relied upon to give a good repeat performance, but there is really no reason for not keeping most tender indoor bulbs (*see pages 64 and 65*) such as amaryllis, begonia tubers and cyclamen corms, for indoor flowering the following year. If they are correctly treated they should perform indoors year after year.

A pot of bulbs in flower is a visual delight in its own right, but a large part of the pleasure is lost if you do not grow them yourself. This is really very simple, and bringing your own bulbs into flower provides an extra thrill, as well as saving money and giving you a much wider choice of plants.

CHOOSING BULBS

You can just wander into your local garden centre at the last minute to see what they have in stock; or you may find yourself buying bulbs on impulse without even knowing what you plan to do with them. But sending for the catalogues of the big bulb producers (advertised in the press) and selecting and ordering your bulbs in good time can become a very pleasant ritual. If you order from a reputable supplier you can be guaranteed good bulbs in perfect condition.

If you buy from retailers, go early in the season (late summer for the majority of spring bulbs) to get the best choice and the freshest bulbs.

ABOVE A little basket of mauve crocuses is the epitome of spring. OPPOSITE A conservatory packed full of daffodils and tulips brings an unrivalled display of colour.

WHAT TO BUY

Select bulbs or corms that are firm and of good size for the type of plant, and that feel heavy for their size. Make sure that they show no sign of mould, damp or damage. Remember to check that bulbs for early indoor flowering have been specially prepared for 'forcing'.

When buying your bulbs, get the bulb fibre or compost for planting them in, and their pots, and anything else you will need, such as charcoal to add to the compost when using pots without drainage, at the same time. Plant the bulbs without delay so that they do not deteriorate through being stored, and to get them off to an early start.

PLANTING BULBS

Always give careful consideration to the pot or container when planting bulbs for indoor displays as this can make or mar the effect you are hoping to create. Hyacinths, daffodils and the other narcissi, tulips and crocuses are normally grown in bowls which have no drainage and although simple and practical plastic bowls are sold for this purpose, an attractive china, glazed earthenware or terracotta pot is much more suitable. The container should be wide and shallow, and preferably non-porous for most situations, as if it is of porous material (such as most terracotta), its damp base may damage table tops and other surfaces. The remedy is to place a saucer or plate under it, which can spoil the effect, or to stand porous containers on a tiled windowsill or kitchen top.

The larger bulbs, such as the various lilies, that are grown as individual specimens, are usually best grown in standard flower pots with saucers and there is a good choice of ornamental versions of these. Ordinary clay pots can also be used, but plastic pots are best hidden by a decorative container that suits the flower and the room.

HYACINTHS

Dutch hyacinths (*Hyancinthus orientalis*) are the most popular indoor hyacinths. Plant from late summer to early autumn, with bulbs of the same variety in one pot. For a good show, the bowl should be just large enough to allow a little space between the bulbs.

The heavily scented, densely packed flower heads of Dutch hyacinths (*Hyacinthus orientalis*) are one of the pleasures of late winter and spring. Careful growing results in compact, sturdy plants, and keeping varieties separate ensures that the plants in one pot are all the same size and in flower at the same time.

2 Seat the bulbs in the compost, close together but not touching – leave a gap of 12mm (½ in) between them. Add more compost, to within about 12mm (½ in) of the rim, and leave the tops of the bulbs showing. Firm in the compost gently around and between the bulbs. Water thoroughly and allow the pot to drain; water sparingly for pots without drainage to avoid waterlogging.

3 Store, wrapped in black polythene, in a very cool place such as a shed or a cellar. Check occasionally that the compost is still moist. Bring into a cool room when shoots are 5–7.5cm (2–3in) high.

1 Make sure the pot is clean, to prevent the risk of mould and infection, and half fill it with damp potting compost or bulb fibre. Position the bulbs on the surface of the compost. When using an odd number of bulbs, start with one central bulb and arrange the rest around it.

TYPE OF COMPOST

Bulb fibre (which is made up of peat or coir fibre, mixed with crushed oyster shells and charcoal) is light and convenient, and cheaper than potting compost. If you do not intend to keep your bulbs after their first flowering it makes a very adequate growing medium. But it contains no nutrients, and is intended for short-term use only. Soil- (or loam-) based potting compost contains a balanced mix of nutrients, and is more akin in structure to the bulbs' natural growing medium. It enables bulbs to develop and replenish themselves after flowering and so is more suitable for bulbs which are to be grown on in future years.

Hippeastrums, usually sold under the name amaryllis (a closely related species) are often grown to flower in winter, but can be planted at intervals, so that they can be in flower almost all year.

A CROCUS POT

A bulbous pot with holes in its sides is perfect for crocuses (*above*). Soak the pot for 24 hours, then put a layer of clay pellets or other drainage material in the bottom of the pot. Put in some damp compost or bulb fibre and position the corms into the holes from the inside, so that their 'noses' are just sticking out on the outside. Firm in, adding more compost as necessary to fill the pot. Add more corms at the top. Cover to keep out the light, taking care not to damage the 'noses'.

Crocuses planted in autumn open their goblet-like flowers in late winter or early spring.

USING A BULB GLASS

Hyacinths are the best plants for a bulb glass. They should be started off in late summer/early autumn, using bulbs that have been prepared for forcing. Fill the glass up to the neck with water and sit the bulb in the container with its base in the water. Keep the glass in a cool, dark place until the leaves begin to show, when the roots should be 7.5–10cm (3–4in) long, then bring it into the warmth and light in gentle stages. Keep the water level topped up so that the bulb base is just in the water especially until the hyacinth's roots have developed.

A bulb glass makes a lovely container for a single hyacinth. The bulb sits neatly within the rim, and its white, fleshy roots fill the rest of the glass, so that the whole of the plant is visible.

DAFFODILS AND TULIPS

Probably the absolute favourites among indoor flowers from bulbs are daffodils (and other popular narcissi) and tulips, and there is such a range of both these plants that it would be possible to have different varieties in flower from early winter until well into the spring. Daffodils are members of the narcissi family that have prominent trumpets. We usually think of them as being yellow, but white and cream varieties also exist. The rest of the family are the plants generally known as 'narcissi', including the bunch-flowered types which are usually highly scented, such as the paper whites. If you want a very early performance from your bulbs, you must make sure that you use bulbs that have been prepared for forcing, as these have been artificially subjected to a cold 'winter' period and can be made ready to begin growing indoors much earlier than normal. They can then be brought into flower very early, or introduced gradually to warmth so that they are only just ahead of their natural seasons. Ordinary, unprepared bulbs can be used if you do not want an unnaturally early show.

EARLY FLOWERS
Small and miniature daffodils such as 'February Gold' and 'Tête-à-Tête' are among the best for growing early indoors. Bulbs planted in late summer can be brought into good light in winter for Christmas flowering (in the northern hemisphere). The scented, bunch-headed narcissi can be forced in glass containers of water and pebbles, with a little charcoal added to keep the water sweet.

Indoor tulips for spring flowering should be planted in mid-autumn.

Early tulips, singles and doubles, are the best types for growing indoors.

Indispensable for brightening up garden borders in early and mid-spring, a pot of tulips can also add colour and cheer to any room in the home.

Bright-yellow, trumpeted daffodils are symbolic of spring and an indoor display is at its best when the bulbs are planted close together.

INDOOR PLANTING

Daffodils and tulips are planted in the same way, except that tulip bulbs are completely covered, while daffodils (*see below*), are planted with their noses showing. Always use scrupulously clean pots and fresh, sterilized compost.

1 Plant daffodils in late summer and tulips from late summer to early autumn, using one variety per bowl. Half fill a clean bowl with damp compost or bulb fibre.

2 Check the height of the compost, using a bulb to measure. When they are planted, the tops of the daffodil bulbs should be just about level with the rim of the bowl (tulip bulbs should be slightly below it). Evenly space the bulbs in the bowl, so that they are close together but are not quite touching. A full bowl will give the best display with a host of flowers.

3 Starting from the middle, add more compost or fibre, pushing it gently between the bulbs with your fingers. Fill the bowl to within 12mm (½in) of the rim.

4 If the bowl or pot has drainage holes, water it well and allow it to drain. Otherwise only water the container lightly.

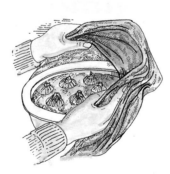

5 Wrap the bowl of bulbs carefully in black polythene and keep covered in a very cool spot. Check regularly to see that the compost is still damp and water if not. Bring daffodils indoors and gradually increase warmth when the shoots are 5cm (2in) high.

FORCING TULIPS

Plant tulips in late summer or very early autumn for indoor flowering. To help their roots to form quickly, you may peel off the outer brown skin. Keep the pots in the coldest part of the garden, covered with a thick layer of soil topped with black polythene, or in the coolest, darkest place you can provide. Check every two weeks to make sure the compost is still damp. Bring the pots into a warm room in early winter but keep them in dim light. When there is about 10cm (4in) growth give the tulips full light and a temperature of about 20°C (68°F). They should then flower around Christmas (in the northern hemisphere). Introduce them only gradually to warmth and light for later flowering.

Tulip bulbs should be completely covered with compost.

'Red Riding Hood' is a bright-red tulip derived from the *Tulipa greigii* species, which is well-known for its maroon or purple-brown veined foliage.

BULBS FOR THE HOME

Bulbs are divided into hardy and tender species. The hardy ones are those that can be grown outside all year in temperate climates – typically the daffodils (*Narcissus* species) and tulips (*Tulipa*), hyacinths (*Hyacinthus*) and crocuses, which can be persuaded to flower indoors in late winter and early spring and which until recent years were the only widely grown houseplant bulbs. It would be a shame to overlook the many tender bulbs that can be grown as houseplants and it is becoming much easier to find them. They include the hippeastrum, better known as amaryllis, usually grown to flower in winter and early spring, but there are many others that provide flowers at other times. Tender bulbs grown as houseplants do not need to be forced. Pot them in soil- (loam-) based compost in pots with good drainage, and keep them in the light at normal temperatures. Water fairly sparingly until shoots appear and then increasingly generously. A few tender bulbs are evergreen and should be kept going all year but most need a cool, dry rest period for a few months once the leaves have died down after flowering.

The hardy daffodils make a good show indoors. Tall varieties such as 'King Alfred' and 'Dutch Master' or shorter-stemmed varieties such as 'Tête à Tête' and 'February Gold' all grow well as houseplants.

The tender hippeastrum is more widely known as amaryllis and produces spectacular lily-like flowers in winter or spring. The true amaryllis is the similar but rarer belladonna lily.

Only the hyacinths sold as 'specially prepared' bulbs are suitable for growing indoors. Their lovely scent is one of the joys of late winter and early spring. Dutch hyacinths are those most usually grown.

HOUSEPLANTS FROM TENDER BULBS

Tender bulbs that can be grown as houseplants include the following:

Babiana stricta (**babiana** or **baboon root**) Has upright stems and leaves, with small, blue, scented flowers growing up the stems in spring. Flowering and planting time can be varied. Flowers in autumn when planted in spring. Hybrids have white, yellow, blue, red or purple flowers. Height 15–30cm (6–12in).

Clivia miniata (**clivia** or **Kaffir lily**) Has flaring, tubular flowers in orange, light red or cream on a sturdy stem surrounded by strappy, glossy, green leaves. Flowers late spring to late summer. Plant in spring. Height 45cm (18in).

Freesia hybrida Freesias have flowers of delicate shape and colour, and exquisite scent, on wiry, branching stems from late winter to late spring. Plant late summer to early winter. Height 30–45cm (12–18in).

Lachenalia aloides (**cape cowslip**) Has sturdy stems hung with rows of narrow, yellow bells with green and red markings. The broad, arching, strap-shaped leaves also have contrast markings. Flowers winter to early spring. Plant in late summer. Height 30cm (12in).

Nerine flexuosa Nerines have whorls of flowers with backward curving petals in pink or white. Flowers on bare stems in autumn are followed by attractive narrow leaves. Plant in late summer. Height 30–60cm (12–24in).

Nerine sariniensis (**Guernsey lily**) Similar to *N. flexuosa*, this nerine species has narrower petals in white, orange or red.

CARE OF TENDER BULBS

All but the evergreen tender bulbs need an annual rest. After they have flowered continue watering until the leaves and flower stems have died down, then cut them off at the base. Store the bulbs – either in their pots or in a box of peat – in a cool, frost-free, dark place without watering. Bring into a warm room and begin to water again in the planting season.

Crocus corms are usually sold by their variety name and are available in many shades of cream and yellow, blue and purple, as well as white. Many of the purple varieties flower later than cream and yellow types.

The bulbous irises can all be grown indoors, and the reticulatas make particularly lovely, softly scented, spring-flowering houseplants. The many named hybrids in this group, are mainly in shades of blue.

Lillies make excellent pot plants. They can be persuaded to flower at any time of year, depending on when they are planted, as long as they are kept cold before planting.

Commonly known as Kaffir lily, clivia will flower year after year if given a cool winter rest. The pot should not be moved once the plant is in bud, or while it is flowering and the plant should not be repotted.

FOLIAGE HOUSEPLANTS

Plants grown mainly for their leaves can form the backbone of a houseplant collection. Many foliage plants are extremely undemanding and very long-lived. They can grow to a good size, or form the most pleasing shapes, and can take up a permanent place in the home.

A mature, large foliage plant such as the ever-popular rubber plant (*Ficus elastica*) or the weeping fig (*Ficus benjamina*) can be at its best displayed alone as a specimen plant, standing in a large handsome container on the floor. Smaller but equally distinctive foliage plants provide perfect specimen plants for tables, sideboards and cupboard tops, and broad windowsills and shelves. These include some very adaptable plants such as Norfolk Island Pine (*Araucaria excelsa*). Foliage plants that creep or trail can be shown off in indoor hanging baskets or trailing down from pots placed on high shelves, and almost any green-leaved foliage plant will act as a foil to a flowering plant. Most rooms in the house have a niche for a foliage plant, and they can be excellent in circulation spaces such as halls and landings where ceilings are often high.

LARGE FOLIAGE PLANTS

Favourites such as the Swiss cheese plant (*Monstera deliciosa*), weeping fig (*Ficus benjamina*), false aralia (*Dizygotheca elegantissima*), yucca and palm, can grow to well over 1m (3ft) high. Growth may be very slow, but eventually you will need a room with a high ceiling. Large entrance halls and landings and half-landings on the stairs can be good places for them as they mature but living rooms are generally ideal in their young days.

Like smaller plants, the large foliage plants can group extremely well when young, with their contrasting leaf shapes setting each other off to great advantage. For this sort of arrangement a raised trough works very well and gives the plants the height they need at this stage of their lives.

ABOVE Contrasting types of foliage can be exploited to the full in a mixed bowl. Here the smooth, shapely leaves of a variegated aspidistra or cast iron plant (*Aspidistra elatior* 'Variegata') are offset by a haze of asparagus fern (*Asparagus densiflorus* 'Sprengeri').
OPPOSITE Specimen plants such as palms and the castor oil plant (*Fatsia japonica*) contrast with the small maidenhair and button ferns.

SMALLER PLANTS

The more modestly sized but bold foliage plants such as mother-in-law's tongue (*Sansevieria trifasciata*) and aspidistra or cast-iron plant (*Aspidistra elatior*), which was favoured by the Victorians and Edwardians for its ability to withstand draughts, poor light and extremes of heat and cold in stuffy rooms heated spasmodically by coal fires, deserve a generous, complementary pot and a focal position – perhaps in an unused fireplace, for example – when reasonably mature. But, especially when young, they too can mix well with other foliage plants in a massed display, perhaps in a trough or a large indoor window box, where they will provide strength and form to contrast with the fluttery ferns or smaller leaved plants.

DISPLAYING IN GLASS

An unusual way to display foliage plants is to grow them in a glass container. This is particularly suitable for smaller moisture-loving plants, as the container creates humidity as well as giving protection from draughts. The plants need very little attention once planted, as they produce their own 'atmosphere' within the container. Round glass containers (carboys) can be bought for bottle gardens, but a container such as a goldfish bowl can be used just as well. The wider the top, the easier it is to manipulate the plants into position when planting, but plants can be grown in glass storage jars or large bottles with small openings, and some will even thrive in the completely self-contained atmosphere of lidded jars with their lids on.

RULES FOR PLANTING

The usual rules for mixed planting in one container apply: the plants must all have the same needs in respect of compost type, light, feeding, temperature and humidity to be grown together successfully. But it is a fiddly business planting up a container of this sort and it is therefore even more important to plan it carefully before you start. And as you will not want to change the arrangement too often, it is best to choose slow-growers, which will not quickly outgrow their space.

1 Make a funnel of thick card and pour a layer of gravel into the clean, dry jar; top with charcoal. Pour in about 5cm (2in) of potting compost.

2 Plan the group before planting. Tease out the roots and place in plants one by one, starting at the centre. You may need to improvise tools.

IMPROVISING TOOLS

The smaller the neck of the bottle, the more difficult it is to plant and maintain the plants inside it without using tools. For planting, a small spoon tied to a cane will hollow out compost, and a cotton reel on a cane can be used to firm plants in. Similarly dining forks attached to a piece of cane can also be useful. For plant maintenance, kitchen scissors can be used to cut back long stems (*shown above*) and a razor blade spliced into the end of a cane can be used for less accessible ones. Other tools can, of course, be improvised as appropriate.

PLANTS FOR GLASS CONTAINERS

There are some interesting small and slow-growing, humidity-loving plants with attractive leaves that are quite suitable for glass containers. These include: aluminium plant (*Pilea cadierei*), young arrowhead vine (*Syngonium podophyllum*), painted leaf (*Begonia rex*), earth stars (*Cryptanthus acaulis* and *C. zonatus*), small-leaved ivies (*Hedera helix*), maidenhair fern (*Adiantum capillus-veneris*), mosaic plant (*Fittonia verschaffeltii* 'Argyroneura Nana'), peperomias and the polka dot plant (*Hypoestes phyllostachya*).

3 Be prepared to funnel in more compost if necessary, then firm in the plants. Place gravel on top of the compost's surface. Water the compost lightly by letting water run down the inside of the glass. This avoids wetting the plants.

WARDIAN CASES

A rectangular glass container such as a fish tank makes a lovely planter for a group of small foliage plants. But special containers with sloping glass lids, known as terrariums or Wardian cases, are also available. Plants in open containers still need watering, but Wardian cases are enclosed systems that almost take care of themselves because moisture within these cases condenses and slides back into the compost.

HYDROCULTURE

Many plants can survive perfectly without compost, using proprietary hydroculture fertilizer granules and tap water. The plant's roots must first be washed completely free of soil in lukewarm water, and the roots trimmed. Expanded clay pellets are used to anchor the roots, and of course there is no point in growing plants this way unless you use glass so that their roots can be seen and admired.

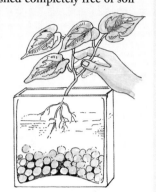

1 Choose healthy foliage plants of varying heights and plan the arrangement on a piece of card that has been cut to the same size and shape as the container.

2 Place gravel, charcoal and damp seed compost in the clean, dry container. Make hollows for plants in the positions as planned, remove plants from pots and tease out the roots. Then firm plants in position.

3 Clean the glass if necessary with a piece of sponge tied to a cane (*above*). Mist-spray the plant arrangement, taking care not to overwet. Put the lid on the container and place in bright, indirect light.

This modern display container is derived from the old-fashioned terrarium – a glass container traditionally used to house humidity-loving plants. Terrariums are still available, and the prayer plants (*Cathalea* species), with their characteristically patterned leaves, are among the plants that grow well in them.

TABLE DECORATION

A table with an arrangement of foliage plants makes an attractive centre-piece or feature in a room and a table with plants on it can bring a hall or passageway to life. The generous surface area of a table top gives scope for more interesting arrangements than narrow shelves, and the plants can be admired from more than one angle. A low coffee table is particularly good for a carefully designed group of plants, enabling the plants to be seen from above as well as from all round. The higher round pedestal tables and side tables are good for showing off trailing plants, which can cascade over the edges of the table. Side tables are usually the best kind to have in a hall.

Old metal sewing machine stands, restored and painted and given suitable tops, pine washstands, with or without their original bowls, and even painted dining room trolleys can be used as substitutes for tables in plant displays.

COFFEE TABLES

For a low central table, it is best to choose low-growing plants of roughly the same height so that you and your guests can see over them when sitting down, and plan the arrangement so that it looks good from all sides. Keeping taller plants to the middle is usually best.

DINING TABLES

For a dining table choose small plants that will not interfere with dining. On a rectangular table a row of neat plants such as mind-your-own-business (*Soleirolia soleirolii*) in matching pots would look pretty, or for a round table a centrally placed bowl of mixed peperomias.

This table arrangement of plants has been designed to be attractive from a variety of viewpoints. From the side, the yellow veins of the croton show up clearly against the red and green leaves underneath.

ABOVE Leaf begonias such as this *Begonia rex* have compact form and richly variegated colouring, making them good plants for table tops.

SUITABLE PLANTS

* Small, compact plants, see page 64
* Trailing plants: *Cissus antarctica* (kangaroo vine), *Ficus pumila* (creeping fig), *Hedera helix* (ivies), *Saxifraga sarmentosa* (mother of thousands), *Syngonium podophyllum* (arrowhead vine), *Tolmiea menziesii* (piggyback plant).
* Larger plants: *Caladium* hybrids (angel's wings), *Carex morrowii* (Japanese sedge), *Chlorophytum comosum* 'Variegatum' (spider plant), *Sansevieria trifasciata* (mother-in-law's tongue).

LEFT With its very dark-green leaves patched with silver, *Pilea cadierei* (also known as the aluminium plant) makes a very attractive plant for a small side table.

ABOVE Growing to about 25cm (12in), the *Calathea crocata* has long, ovate leaves and orange-red flowers appearing from orange bracts and makes a pretty focal point.

WALL TABLES

Tables against a wall can take taller plants. The style can be formal, perhaps with a trailing plant at each end and three matching compact plants between them, or informal, with a balanced group showing off different types of foliage. One large plant can be just as arresting as a group – for example, a single, large trailing vine spilling over the front edge of a small table. Side tables which are not used for other purposes are a good place for groups of plants and objects, such as a collection of pebbles, a pair of candlesticks, or a display of driftwood or ornaments.

PRACTICAL POINTS

Apart from making sure that your plants will not interfere with the use of the table, there are other points to bear in mind. You may need to protect the table top from damage caused by the plant containers, and you will need to make sure that the table is standing in a safe place where it will not get knocked over as people come and go. Choose plants that are suitable for the light conditions, and do not expose any but the toughest plants to draughts in halls. When using trailing plants, make sure that the container gives them height, so that they can trail effectively.

TRAILING AND CASCADING PLANTS

Foliage plants that trail or cascade can be shown off to the full in hanging bowls or baskets, or trailing down from pots placed on high shelves. The old trick of filtering out a less than perfect view by growing trailing plants in pots on a shelf fixed across the top of the window so that the greenery trails down the glass is well tried and tested. Trailers can grow down from pots placed on small shelves or ornamental wall brackets, and they are perfect for high windows, which allow them to tumble down the wall below the sill. Smaller trailing plants can be grown around other plants in a grouped arrangement, where they can fill in the gaps between the plants and spill over the edges of the container, or they can be planted to cover the base and pot edges of large specimen plants. And plants with arching stems are ideal for display in a pot on a tall pedestal.

**A CHOICE
OF EASY PLANTS**
All these plants flourish in normal room temperatures unless otherwise stated.

Asparagus **'Sprengeri' (emerald feather)** This is the larger, more common, and more luxuriant of the two popular asparagus ferns (which are not, in fact, true ferns) – the other being *A.* 'Meyeri', the plume fern. The hanging stems of emerald feathers are covered with a froth of green needles and quickly grow to 90–120cm (3–4ft). Plume fern has shorter and more upright arching stems to 60cm (2ft).

Light: Semi-shade.

Temperature: Winter minimum of 8°C (48°F).

High humidity is needed, especially when the air is warm. Feed every two weeks from spring to autumn.

EASY TRAILING PLANTS

Undemanding trailing plants include: *Callisia elegans* (striped inch plant); *Epipremnum pinnatum* 'Aureum' , often sold as *Scindapsus aureus* (devil's ivy); *Mikania ternata* (plush/velvet vine); *Nephrolepis exaltata* 'Bostoniensis' (Boston fern); *Oplismenus hirtellus* (basket grass); *Pellaea rotundifolia* (button fern); *Peperomia scandens* and *P. s.* 'Variegatum' (cupid peperomia/hanging peperomia); *Plectranthus australis* and *P. oertendahlii* (Swedish ivy); *Tradescantia fluminensis* (tradescantia/inch plant/wandering Jew); *Zebrina pendula* (silvery inch plant/wandering sailor).

With its trailing habit and heart-shaped leaves, sweetheart plant (*Philodendron scandens*) is perfect for a hanging basket. Here it is balanced visually by a sword fern (*Nephrolepis cordifolia*) a small-leaved trailing ivy (*Hedera helix*) and the white-and-green leaved candle plant (*Plectranthus coleoides* 'Marginatus') – all equally easy plants to grow.

OPPOSITE The trouble-free purple heart (*Setcreasea pallida* 'Purple Heart') can quickly become straggly, but it is easy to grow replacement plants from cuttings.

ABOVE With its waxy, golden green-edged leaves, *Hoya carnosa* 'Tricolor' is a striking climbing plant.

ABOVE Swedish ivy (*Plectranthus oertendahlii*) is a vigorous and undemanding houseplant. It trails well, and can be pinched out at the tips to keep it bushy.

Chlorophytum comosum **(spider plant)** This well-known plant has arching green leaves and is best known in its striped forms *C. c .* 'Variegatum' and *C. c.* 'Vittatum'. Grow it where its white runners (up to 75cm (30in) long), with their little plantlets, can hang freely.

Light: Bright, indirect light.

Temperature: Winter low of 7°C (45°F).

Feed weekly from spring to autumn and repot as soon as the roots fill the pot.

Ficus pumila **(creeping fig)** A relative of the rubber plant which has small, glossy, heart-shaped leaves when young. Its shoots grow up to 30cm (12in) per year. The variety 'Sonny' has white-edged leaves.

Light: Semi-shade.

Temperature: Winter minimum of 10°C (50°F).

Give moisture and humidity.

Glechoma hederacea **'Variegata' (creeping variegated ground ivy)** This has white-splashed, scalloped leaves and grows best in cooler rooms. It grows well as a trailer and its stems can reach up to 1.8m (6ft) if not kept trimmed.

Light: Bright, indirect light.

Temperature: Not more than 13°C (55°F) in winter.

Needs moist compost, and a weekly summer feed.

Philodendron scandens **(sweetheart plant)** This popular plant has glossy, heart-shaped leaves. It can be trained as a climber, but spreads and trails beautifully, with shoots growing 60–90cm (2–3ft) in a year.

Light: Good, indirect light. Tolerates periods in shade.

Temperature: Never more than 24°C (75°F).

Water generously from spring to autumn and feed weekly during the summer.

Saxifraga stolonifera **(mother of thousands)** This plant has a mound of round, hairy leaves and produces wiry, pinkish runners up to 90cm (3ft) long threaded with numerous little plantlets. The variety 'Tricolor' has variegated leaves marked with white and flushed with pink in patches.

Light: Good, indirect light.

Temperature: Winter minimum of 10°C (50°F).

Water from below, fairly generously in summer and more sparingly in winter. Feed every two weeks in summer.

Setcreasea pallida **(purple heart)** This tolerant plant has long, narrow, purple leaves with a velvety bloom. The upright stems of young plants soon grow long and can become straggly, but it is easy to grow replacement plants from cuttings.

Light: Full sun.

Temperature: Normal summer room temperature. Not below 7–10°C (45–50°F) in winter.

Water moderately in summer, sparingly in winter.

CLIMBING HOUSEPLANTS

In the wild, climbing plants climb up, sprawl over, or twine round a host by means of aerial roots, sprawling stems or curling tendrils. So in the home they need to be given some means of support. Plants with tendrils will soon cling to the support by their tendrils, but other types need to be tied in. Such climbers can equally well be left to their own devices, given no support and not tied in, and grown as trailing plants – it is all just a question of training. Most climbers will happily grow up a suitable cane, but plants with aerial roots can be grown up moss poles and other climbers are often trained into ornamental shapes or up a trellis.

Climbing foliage plants include some of the most tolerant plants, and can be used in many decorative ways. Stately, larger leaved plants such as elephant's ear (*Philodendron hastatum*), which produces large, fleshy, aerial roots, make a strong statement and are often best in isolation, growing slowly to great height over the years. Scramblers such as grape ivy (*Cissus rhombifolia*) will travel a long way in a short time and can be trained in all sorts of styles.

BELOW Arrowhead vine (*Syngonium podophyllum*) is a fleshy-leaved climber with aerial roots for training up a moss pole. Many varieties have variegated leaves, including white-veined 'White Butterfly'.

SELECTED PLANTS

The following are some of the easiest climbing plants:

Cissus antarctica (**kangaroo vine**) This has a mass of tooth-edged, glossy green leaves and is tolerant of poor light. As a young plant it is normally grown up a group of canes, but when older it can be trained over a trellis. It is vigorous and can be trimmed back at any time of year to keep it within bounds.

C. discolor (**begonia vine**) This variety has pointed leaves that are a mixture of colours on top and deep-dark red underneath. It can become straggly.

× *Fatshedera lizei* (**ivy tree**) The leaves are like large ivy leaves. A variegated form, × *F. l.* 'Variegata', is available but this is less tolerant.

Hedera canariensis (**Canary island ivy**) This undemanding plant is usually grown in its variegated form 'Gloire de Marengo' which has green and white leaves, is easily trained as a climber and very good for draughty halls. It must have reasonably cool conditions, with adequate light.

Nephthytis 'Emerald Gem' (**goose foot plant**) Among the easiest of the plants with aerial roots, it has big, spade-shaped leaves and is good for growing up moss poles. It needs shade and moisture.

Philodendron hastatum (**elephant's ear**) Reaches 6m (20ft) in a greenhouse but is a modest 1.5m (5ft) in a pot. It needs a big moss pole and a position in semi-shade.

Rhoicissus rhomboidea (**grape ivy**) A long-lived plant with a mass of glossy, dark-green, tooth-edged leaves that will tolerate some shade but does best in a fairly bright light. It needs plenty of room and grows well over a trellis or round a doorway.

RIGHT Canary Island ivy (see below also) is a good plant for halls and landings as it likes fairly cool growing conditions and indirect light and will tolerate quite poor light. It must be given plenty of humidity, especially when the surrounding air is warm.

OTHER CLIMBING PLANTS

✳ **Hedera helix** hybrids (small and large-leaved ivies), including colourful *H.* 'Goldheart' (syn. 'Jubilee') which has small, yellow-splashed leaves. Good in unheated rooms.

✳ **Scindapsus aureus** or **Epipremnum aureum** (devil's ivy), a fast grower with patterned leaves, for canes, trellis or moss pole in bright or dim light.

✳ **Gynura sarmentosa** (velvet plant) has hairy, purple leaves and grows very fast given plenty of light. Often grown as a trailer, it is easily trained.

LEFT AND BELOW Mermaid vine (*Rhoicissus rhomboidea* – 'Ellen Danica' and also known as *Cissus rhombifolia* 'Ellen Danica') (left) and the variegated Canary Island ivy (*Hedera canariensis* 'Variegata' and *H. c.* 'Gloire de Marengo') (below) are two of the most amenable foliage plants and can be trained in a variety of ways.

BELOW Trained up canes, a kangaroo vine (*Cissus antarctica*) soon develops into a substantial specimen for a large pot. The plant is at home in all sorts of decorative styles and is easy to grow in ordinary room temperatures, preferably cool in winter.

FLOOR-STANDING PLANTS

The big, architectural plants really come into their own standing alone displayed as specimen plants in large pots on the floor. The container you use makes all the difference. For large plants, it is usually best to have a container which is one quarter to a third the height of the pot, in a shape and style that both flatters the plant and complements the furniture and decor of the room. As the plant grows you will need to repot it into a pot one size larger from time to time to prevent it from becoming pot-bound and this creates an opportunity to change the cache pot or container to keep it in proportion with the plant. Very large plants that are too big to be repotted should be top dressed – the top 2.5–5cm (1–2in) of their compost being removed annually and replaced with fresh compost, which provides a supply of nutrients and aerates the compost.

Smaller plants with bold forms and patterned leaves, such as the easy coleus plants and more demanding crotons (*Codiaeum variegatum pictum* and varieties), also look good standing on the floor where you can look down on their leaves, and these plants benefit from being planted in groups of two or three varieties together to show off their contrasting leaf colouring. You can also make a floor group of assorted foliage plants of differing heights with a mixture of leaf shapes, colours and forms.

PRACTICAL POINTS

There is often least light at floor level. Luckily there are plenty of suitable foliage plants – the many calatheas and marantas, for example – that need shade, and for others you can raise the plants' level by using a planting trough on legs. Standing plants on the floor is ideal for attic rooms with low windows, or for rooms with overhead lighting, where bright light reaches down to floor level.

Too many pots standing on the floor can be unwelcome when you have to clean round them – a single container is often the best solution in all but a conservatory room. Alternatively, a low platform on coasters, that can be moved for cleaning, will enable you to make a floor-level grouping of plants.

ABOVE The well-known castor oil plant or Japanase aralia (*Fatsia japonica*), will thrive almost anywhere except in direct sun – in a sheltered position, it is even hardy enough to survive outside.

With its finger-like lobes, this plant can make an attractive feature in halls and landings, and also to rooms that are not overheated in winter. There is also a variegated form which is slightly smaller than the all-green type shown here, and has pretty, white-tipped leaves.

Rubber plants (*Ficus elastica*) are good, bold specimens to stand in pots on the floor. The variegated forms, such as 'Tricolor' or 'Doescheri', are becoming more popular than the all-green types but they can be more temperamental.

THE BEST AREAS

Plants can be positioned on the floor in a corner, next to a big window or glass door, in an unused fireplace, in a hall, near the front door, on a landing or turn in the stairs.

PLANTS TO CHOOSE

Some of the best plants to stand on the floor are:

***Dizygotheca elegantissima* (false aralia)** A plant with masses of many-fingered, saw-edged leaves that throw a good shadow when well-lit.

***Fatsia japonica* (castor-oil plant or Japanese aralia)** Has glossy, palmate leaves; young plants grow very quickly.

***Ficus benjamina* (weeping fig)** A small tree with fluttering leaves on weeping branches.

***Ficus elastica* 'Decora' (rubber plant)** Sturdy and shapely with big, bold, prominently ribbed, shiny leaves. The variety *F. e.* 'Robusta' has bigger leaves still. Do not overwater.

***Monstera deliciosa* (Swiss cheese plant)** This plant has very large, leathery leaves, which develop holes like Swiss cheese as they grow.

***Schefflera actinophylla* (umbrella plant)** With glossy, pointed leaflets fanning out from around tops of stiff, radiating stems. Can reach 1.8m (6ft).

***Yucca elephantipes* (yucca or spineless yucca)** Develops a straight trunk with strappy, palm-like leaves; likes to spend warm summers outside.

LEFT The yucca (*Yucca elephantipes*) grows up to 1.5m (5ft) high and has a distinctly oriental look. It needs good light and fairly cool winter conditions, and if well cared for it will eventually produce white flowers.

LEFT The Swiss cheese plant (*Monstera deliciosa*) needs a big tub and strong support. This is best provided by a moss pole covered with netting, so that the plant's aerial roots can be tucked into the moss, which should be mist-sprayed regularly.

Umbrella tree (*Heptapleurum arboricola*) grows quickly to a height of 1.5–1.8m (5–6ft) to form a bushy plant. Its leaves consist of 6 to 8 leaflets radiating on parasol 'spokes' from the tips of leaf-stalks. This plant is also sold as *Schefflera arboricola*.

BERRIED, FRUITING AND INSECTIVOROUS PLANTS

Some of the most decorative and curious houseplants are grown not for their flowers but for their fruits or berries, or even for their peculiar eating habits. Fruiting plants can give double value, sometimes having beautiful, fragrant flowers as well, but in general, plants with attractive berries, such as the bead plant (*Nertera depressa*), have negligible flowers.

Most insectivorous and fruiting plants need extra care – the insectivores all require a protected environment and high humidity, and fruiting plants – especially those with edible fruit, such as miniature orange, lemon and kumquat – need a conservatory or at least an airy, sunny room, and do not produce fruit without the right amount of warmth, light and humidity. Some of the best ornamental fruiting plants, however, are easily grown as annuals from seed each year such as ornamental peppers (*Capsicum annuum*).

ABOVE Ornamental peppers (*Capsicum annuum*) are cheerful plants for autumn and winter with their brightly coloured fruits. They do best in direct light where several of the plants arranged together will make a colourful show.

PLANTS WITH FRUIT OR BERRIES

Fruit and berry-bearing plants for the home include:

***Capsicum annuum* (ornamental peppers)** These plants are grown as annuals. They come in many colours, from red and yellow to white, purple and black, all starting off as green. Sow the seed in spring, cover the seed tray and keep at a temperature of 21°C (70°F). Germination takes about two weeks. Pot up as the plants grow and pinch them out at the tips to make them bushy and fruitful. Give plenty of humidity, water well and feed once a fortnight as peppers appear.

***Citrus mitis* (calamondin, Panama or ornamental orange)** A dwarf orange tree that grows slowly to a height of 1m (3½ft). Well-watered in summer, and given plenty of light all year and a cool, 13°C

ABOVE Kumquats (*Fortunella margarita*) are highly decorative though rather temperamental. Given plenty of light, warmth and moisture they will produce attractive fruit.

(55°F), winter rest, it produces white, scented, waxy flowers and small, edible fruit. Even if it fails to flower it is an attractive, bushy, evergreen shrub. The dwarf lemon or Meyer lemon, *C. limon* 'Meyeri', is similar but bears small, ornamental lemon fruits.

***Ficus deltoidea* (mistletoe fig)** Has grey-gold, sometimes red-flushed, berries borne singly on little stems sprouting from the leaf-joints. Its leaves are small, oval and dark green and the bush is slow-growing – usually to about 45–75cm (18–30in) high and 45cm (18in) across, although it can grow much bigger in a tub. The plant will stand a winter low of 10°C (50°F).

Solanum capsicastrum (**winter cherry**) This plant has nothing to do with cherries and its shining, round berries turning from green through yellow to orange or red during the winter are actually poisonous. Do not overwater, and keep in a fairly cool room at 10–15.5°C (50–60°F) but in very bright light. Jerusalem cherry (*S. pseudo-capsicum*) is similar, but with larger berries.

INSECTIVOROUS PLANTS

Insectivorous plants are of three main types: pitcher plants, sticky-leaved plants and fly traps.

Darlingtonia californica (**pitcher plant** or **cobra lily**) Looks just like a cluster of snakes. Its nectar attracts insects, which then become trapped in the plant's 'pitcher'. It needs good, indirect light,

normal summer temperatures and a cool 7–10°C (45–50°F) in winter, and very high humidity and generous watering especially in summer.

Nepenthes coccinea, another pitcher plant, has broad, arching leaves with 'pitchers' hanging from the tips, and is ideal for a hanging basket.

Sarracenia purpurea, (**huntsman's cup**), *S. flava*, (**huntsman's horn**) and the hybrid *S.* × *catesbaei* all have upright, horn-like 'pitchers'.

Other insectivorous plants are sticky-leaved sundews *Drosera binata* and *D. capensis*, which trap and digest insects with the juices secreted by their hairy leaves and *Dionaea muscipula* (**Venus fly-trap**) with its snapping, tooth-fringed leaves.

BELOW The yellow American pitcher plant *Sarracenia flava* is known as huntsman's horn and is hardy in temperate climates.

LEFT *Sarracenia leucophylla* has purple veining and a decoratively frilled cap to its deep horn-shaped pitcher. Like all pitcher plants, it produce enzymes which enable it to digest the insects attracted to its pitcher-like traps. Unlike many, however, it is very tall (about 75cm (30in) high) and can digest large insects such as blue bottles.

Bead plant (*Nertera depressa*) is usually grown as a pot plant for its bright autumn and winter berries. It needs bright light, cool air and plenty of summer moisture. If it is given a dry, late winter rest, followed by a spring and summer spent outdoors, it will produce its shiny 'beads' year after year.

Venus fly trap (*Dionaea muscipula*) is one of the most readily available of the insectivorous plants. It needs a light, moist, well-drained compost and a sunny position but also plenty of humidity.

PALMS, FERNS AND BROMELIADS

Palms, ferns and bromeliads are not, of course, related, but they all provide most distinctive foliage and have something exotic about them.

Most palms grown as houseplants are tropical or subtropical plants that require warmth and humidity and bright but filtered light, although there are some, such as the small, parlour palm (*Chamaedorea elegans* also known as *Neanthe bella*), and the much larger kentia palm (*Howea forsteriana*) that famously tolerate ordinary, fluctuating living-room conditions.

Ferns have been popular since Victorian days, when they were collected and housed in glass cases or in glass ferneries built on outdoor balconies. They can look exotically redolent of the jungle, or light and fragile.

Bromeliads are air plants, growing in the wild on other plants or on rocks and taking their nourishment from the air and from organic debris, though a few root in shallow soil. Many adapt to being grown in pots.

FINDING AND BUYING THE PLANTS

While palms and ferns and some types of bromeliad are just coming back into fashion after a period of neglect, many bromeliads have only recently been introduced to cultivation as houseplants.

Many of these plants have to be sought out, as only the most popular are widely available. Some palms, especially young ones, can be bought from nurseries and garden centres and even the plant sections of large supermarkets and chain stores, but others will have to be obtained from specialist houseplant growers.

Commoner ferns and bromeliads can also be found in many garden centres and other shops, but the more unusual specimens of these plants too have to be obtained from specialist growers.

ABOVE Sago palm (*Cycas revoluta*) is also known as Japanese sago palm and Japanese fern palm. Although it is not a true palm, it is often sold as one in garden centres. Its strong, fan-like fronds sprout from a conical base which is part of its attraction. The plant needs warmth and humidity and normally grows only one new leaf a year, eventually reaching a height of about 75cm (2.5ft) with a spread of 50cm (20in).
OPPOSITE The bamboo palm (*Chamaedorea seifrizii*) has dozens of cane-like stems and grows to a height of 1.8m (6ft) or more.

GROWING PALMS, FERNS AND BROMELIADS

A palm takes dedication and time to produce and is a long-term investment, to be chosen with care and looked after equally carefully.

Ferns from temperate regions are often less than ideal as houseplants, as they require cooler conditions than centrally heated homes can offer, but the numerous tropical and sub-tropical ferns flourish in the temperatures we prefer for ourselves as long as they are given plenty of humidity and not subjected to sudden temperature changes.

Many bromeliads can be grown in pots indoors as exotic tropical plants and although they are grown as foliage plants some occasionally produce spectacular flowers. Others can be grown on stones and driftwood, or up moss poles, and some are well-suited for hanging baskets.

GROWING AND DISPLAYING PALMS

Palms are very much associated with ideas of elegance and splendour, and of exotic lands. They make us think of Palm Sunday, oases in the hot, dry desert and palm-fringed beaches of white sand, or of the palm courts and palm court orchestras of fashionable watering places of days gone by. In Victorian and Edwardian times the most demanding and largest palms were grown in glass houses, where they could be given the warmth and lush humidity they needed, but the surprisingly resilient fronds of the most tolerant species swayed over the comings and goings in hotel foyers and restaurants in all sorts of public rooms. The entrance halls and drawing rooms of late nineteenth- and early twentieth-century homes were also often graced with parlour palms.

DISPLAYING PALMS TODAY

As simpler styles replaced the opulence and clutter and dim light of Victorian and Edwardian interiors, palms went out of fashion. But they have found their way back into our homes again in interiors of a very different style. With its well-defined fronds and its stark but graceful shape, a palm is an outstanding plant, which makes a striking feature, and one which is especially well-suited to a large, bright, plainly furnished and decorated interior.

The Canary Island date palm (*Phoenix canariensis*) makes a lovely specimen plant. When young the plant looks well on a pedestal table or palm stand, and as it matures – becoming 1.2–1.8m (4–6ft) high in time – it needs a spot on the floor where its upright, arching fronds and stiff, dark-green leaflets can be properly admired.

LEFT Palms work well in formal pairs. A kentia palm (*Howea forsteriana*) either side of an arched opening lends symmetry and dignity. Kentia palms can eventually reach ceiling height to become fine floor-standing specimens with regal, arching stems.

LEFT A small palm blends well with other foliage plants. Standing on a broad windowsill, this Canary Island palm (*Phoenix canariensis*) casts light shadows on the wall beside it.

LEFT Although kentia palms (*Howea forsteriana*) eventually become large plants they retain the lightness and grace shown by this small young specimen. A window position is ideal for winter, but some shade from summer sun is needed.

POTS AND PALM STANDS

Traditionally, palms were displayed on ceramic palm stands, with the palm planted in an ornamental jardinière balanced on top of a matching pedestal. Displaying them in this way (using original or reproduction palm stands – both expensive) is perfect for a room in a period house decorated in period style. But it could also successfully supply an unusual feature in an otherwise simple, modern interior. Borrowing this idea, any pedestal or pedestal table provides a good means of giving prominence to the smaller palms. But a large palm generally looks at its best standing on the floor in a pot or cache pot of good quality, and in any case it will be too heavy to be raised on any kind of stand. Containers can be patterned porcelain, glazed earthenware, brass or copper, basketware, or even plain, well-made plastic planters, depending on the setting.

OASIS OR JUNGLE

Palms grow in two rather extreme situations – in arid deserts and in lush-green jungles. Either of these can be expressed in the way the plants are displayed. Palms in a bare room, with polished or varnished wooden floors, echo the idea of plants growing in a barren, desert landscape, but palms growing with other foliage plants, perhaps in a room with a green carpet or a green-patterned wallpaper, bring out the tropical jungle theme. This can also be achieved in miniature with a group of foliage plants such as leaf begonias, selaginellas and small ferns grown in a glass case with a small, young palm such as *Chamaedora elegans* or *Microcoelum weddeliana*.

LEFT The way in which a palm is displayed can change its appearance. Standing on the floor in a plain blue pot and lit by a spotlight from below, the Canary Island palm casts dramatic shadows which almost double the plant's impact.

REFLECTIONS AND LIGHTING

Perhaps more than any other plant, palms lend themselves to creating shadows and reflections. For example, a palm standing in an alcove that is lined with a mirror creates a stunning effect, and one each side of a fireplace reflected in this way is doubly stunning. The shadows cast by a palm's fronds can pattern a plain wall in a most dramatic way. Spotlights create a good strong light for bold shadows, but generate heat so must not be positioned too close to the plant. Lighting the plant from below creates shadows on the ceiling as well as the walls. A plain blind (as opposed to a curtain) provides a good, smooth surface for shadows.

PALMS AS HOUSEPLANTS

In the wild, many – though not all – palms grow to great heights, but in the main they are slow-growing plants and can remain at living-room size for many years. These are not plants for impatient indoor gardeners. New fronds unfurl in a leisurely way at the rate of only two or three a year. In many of the palms grown as houseplants several fronds are produced from ground, or compost, level, whereas the very large palms, which generally require extremely high temperatures – the date palms (*Phoenix* species) for example – have a single stem (the trunk) with a flourish of fronds at the top. A frond is really a sort of compound leaf and each apparent leaf is really a leaflet, forming part of the whole frond. In each frond, all the growth develops from a single growth point, known as the terminal bud, and if the bud is damaged the whole frond is affected. If you cut a stem it will not re-grow. Palms are among the few plants that grow best in relatively small containers.

GENERAL CARE

The most popular palms are adaptable specimens. They like to have a winter rest in cooler conditions, although not normally in temperatures below about 10°C (50°F) but they tolerate central heating. They prefer good but not strong light, especially when young (when in the wild they would be growing in the shade of other, taller plants) but they can survive in quite dim corners. They do dislike draughts and any sudden changes (although some prefer a regular slight drop in temperature at night).

They grow best if their roots are allowed to fill the pot, and should not be repotted unnecessarily. A soil- (loam-) based potting compost is needed, with plenty of drainage material at the bottom of the pot. During the summer, or in warm rooms, they need plenty of watering, but in lower temperatures the compost should be allowed to dry out a little between waterings. The plants should never be allowed

ABOVE Bamboo palm (*Rhapsis excelsa*) is a spreading fan palm.

to become waterlogged and must not stand with their pots in any excess water that has drained out. They should be regularly fed in summer.

Palms are very sensitive to chemicals, and will be damaged if exposed to aerosol sprays. If you need to treat them with insecticides, ensure that these are suitable for palms.

Areca palm (*Chrysalidocarpus lutescens*) rejoices under many names. It may be sold as butterfly palm, yellow palm, golden feather palm, yellow butterfly palm, cane palm and golden cane palm. It has slim, upright stems of broad, waving fronds and is a relatively fast-growing palm which can hold its own in the most austere setting. It comes from Madagascar and enjoys temperatures of 13–16°C (55–61°F) in winter and up to 27°C (80°F) in summer.

BELOW Palms are among the plants known as 'architectural' plants. They are long-lived and introduce permanency to a room. Two well-known palms are the kentia palm (*Howea forsteriana*, earlier known as *Kentia forsteriana*), of palm court fame, which creates a dramatic feature (left), and the parlour palm (*Chamaedorea elegans* and also known as *Neanthe bella*), which has a feathery outline (right).

HUMIDITY

Humidity is normally appreciated by palms, and they should be mist-sprayed frequently in warm rooms. They can also be stood on a tray of wet pebbles to keep the atmosphere humid. The fronds should be cleaned from time to time by being wiped with a cloth that has been wrung out in tepid water.

HOUSEPLANT PALMS

Palms are divided into bamboo-like cane palms, fan palms, which have segmented fronds fanning round from the ends of the stalks, feather palms whose fronds consist of feather-like leaflets on either side of the midrib, and fishtail palms whose fronds have fish-shaped leaflets. Some of the best for houseplants are:

Canary Island date palm (*Phoenix canariensis*); coconut palm (*Cocos nucifera*); European fan palm (*Chamaerops humilis*); kentia palm (*Howea forsteriana*), sentry palm (*H. belmoreana*) and parlour palm (*Chamaedora elegans* syn. *Neanthe bella*), which all need lower temperatures at night; and windmill palm (*Trachycarpus fortunei*).

LEFT Palms are the perfect specimen plants for an elegant setting. The Chinese fan palm (*Livingstonia chinensis*) is at home in a period room, standing in a broad alcove and spreading up to the ceiling but the plant might be too dramatic for a smaller room.

OTHER PALMS TO GROW

✳ Cane palms, 1.5–3m (5–10ft): *Chamaedorea seifrizii* (reed palm); *Chamaedorea erumpens* (bamboo palm); *Chrysalidocarpus lutescens* (cane, or golden feather palm).

✳ Fan palms: *Livistona chinensis* (Chinese fan palm) 1.2–3m (4–10ft); *Rhapis excelsa* (little lady palm/bamboo fan palm/miniature fan palm) 90–150cm (3–5ft); *Washingtonia filifera* (desert fan palm) 2.4m (8ft).

✳ Feather palm: *Phoenix roebelenii* (pygmy date palm/miniature date palm) 90–120cm (3–4ft).

✳ Fishtail palms: *Caryota mitis* (Burmese/clustered/tufted fishtail palm) 1.5–2.4m (5–8ft); *Syagus weddelliana* (syn. *Cocos weddelliana*) (dwarf cocos palm) under 1.8m (6ft).

GROWING AND DISPLAYING FERNS

The Victorians grew ferns, collected from all over the empire, in glazed ferneries or in special glass cases (terrariums or Wardian cases). Under glass the ferns could enjoy each other's company in a humid environment completely protected from draughts, smoke and fumes. Bottle gardens and Wardian cases are still available, and are excellent for small ferns. The ferns in them remain green and healthy and look natural and pretty, yet demand little attention. Many garden centres now sell a selection of ferns to grow in this way, making choosing the right plants very simple.

Whether in glass containers or not, ferns lend themselves well to being displayed in groups, as each fern can enjoy the moisture transpired through the fronds of its neighbours, so that to some extent a 'mini climate' is created around them. But the other plants in the group need not all be ferns – a fern or two can be used to soften a group of foliage plants with their contrasting feathery forms, and ferns with arching fronds are ideal for display in a hanging basket arrangement. The larger ferns, however, and those with bold foliage, can look very commanding displayed on their own.

SPECIMEN FERNS

The bird's nest fern, (*Asplenium nidus*), with its broad, glossy leaves, about 8cm (3in) wide and 45cm (18in) long, makes an excellent plant for a pot standing alone on a small table. As it needs shade, it is suitable for a position away from the window.

The Boston fern (*Nephrolepis exaltata* 'Bostoniensis') and other varieties of this species make perfect specimen plants. Their long, arching fronds of up to 60cm (2ft) long make them ideal for display on a stand or in a big pot on a small, high table, perhaps made of cane or bamboo.

RIGHT The light-green leaves of a bird's nest fern (*Asplenium nidus*) stand out brightly against the dark foliage of the kangaroo vine (*Cissus antarctica*) and are further contrasted by the shape and colouring of the variegated ivy *Hedera helix* 'Eva'.

The sedately arching fronds of a mature lace fern (*Nephrolepis exaltata* 'Whitmonii') are displayed at their best on a plant stand. All the popular nephrolepis ferns make good specimen plants.

The architectural appearance of this staghorn fern (*Platycerium bifurcatum*) makes a striking and eye-catching display.

Other distinctive ferns for a stand include the palm fern (*Blechnum gibbum*), brake fern (*Pteris quadriaurita*), bronze fern (*Didymochlaena truncaulata*), shield fern (*Polystichum acrostichoides*), hare's foot fern (*Polypodium aureum*) and *Microlepia* ferns.

FERNS FOR A BASKET
Many ferns have arching stems and look good in hanging baskets. The compact button fern (*Pellaea rotundifolia*) and smaller maidenhair fern (*Adiantum raddianum*) are pretty in a small basket, while the vigorous climbing fern (*Stenochlaena tenuifolia)* and the Boston fern and feather fern (*Nephrolepis exaltatal* 'Bostoniensis' and *N. e.* 'Whitmanii') are all perfect for a large hanging container.

FERNS WITHOUT POTS
The popular staghorn fern (*Platycerium bifurcatum*) (*see left*) is an epiphyte – a surface-growing plant that does not require a depth of soil – and grows well without a pot. Small ferns can also be grown without pots, either planted in peaty compost in a collection in a glass fern case, or grown in a fern column (*see below*).

A FERN PLAQUE
The unusual-looking staghorn fern (*Platycerium bifurcatum*), which has eye-catching fronds divided like a stag's horns, can be displayed mounted on a plaque of cork bark or a slice of log, with a chain for hanging (*above*). Wrap the fern's roots in sphagnum moss lined with peat and attach it with twine or plastic-coated wire to the bark. Water the plant – frequently at first to keep it constantly wet, and then once a week – by dipping the whole plaque in water, then allowing the surplus to drain away.

ABOVE Boston fern (*Nephrolepis exaltata* 'Bostoniensis') is justly popular as a handsome specimen that tolerates a range of conditions.

FERN COLUMNS
A fern column is a striking way to display tiny ferns. Make a tube, about 10cm (4in) in diameter and about 45cm (18in) long, from chicken wire. Splay out the base, and cement or glue it to a large plant saucer. Using a funnel, pour in a layer of well-drained, soil- (loam-) based potting compost with` added peat and poke the roots of the ferns into it through the mesh with your fingers, spreading them out and firming them in. Continue in stages up the pole. Tweezers can be used to handle the plants.

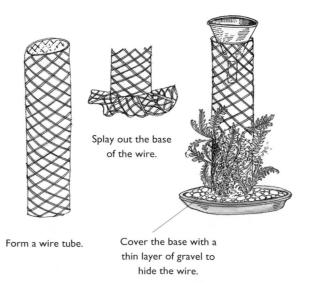

Form a wire tube.

Splay out the base of the wire.

Cover the base with a thin layer of gravel to hide the wire.

FERNS AS HOUSEPLANTS

Ferns are not difficult to grow but draughts, dry air and extremes of temperature are injurious to them. A fern that is pampered and protected from these threats will reward its owner with a wealth of luxuriant green fronds all year round. There are many species of tropical and subtropical ferns, but there are also many ferns that are native to areas with temperate climates. These are well-suited to cooler parts of the house and will not survive in rooms that are too well-heated. Ferns from tropical parts are naturally at home in warmer air and are better suited to centrally heated rooms.

All ferns thrive on moisture and need to be given high humidity. In living rooms this usually means standing them on trays of damp pebbles, or putting each fern's pot in a larger pot and packing the gap with peat that is kept moist, and mist-spraying regularly with tepid, soft water unless the humidity of the whole room is kept high through the use of a humidifier. Providing the right compost is also important, as ferns in general are forest or woodland plants, and have tender, delicate roots adapted to the light forest soil, rich in leaf mould and decayed vegetable matter.

COMPOST AND MOISTURE

A light, moisture-retaining compost is the first requirement for ferns. But this must be freely draining, so that their roots are never waterlogged. A compost based on peat, or fibrous peat substitute, containing plenty of fine sand and small, sharp stones is best. The compost should never be allowed to dry out, and this may mean giving a little water everyday in a warm, dry atmosphere.

LIGHT

Ferns grow in moist, shady places. But this does not mean that they need no light. Their normal condition is dappled light, and light levels that are too low cause poor growth and yellowing fronds. Give ferns a position near a window that gets morning or late afternoon sun, or in good light within the room. Keep them away from strong sunlight, particularly in summer, as it will soon make them lose their intense colouring and turn them a pallid or greyish-green, and it can also scorch their fronds, making them brown and dry round the edges.

Ferns can be kept in dim light as long as they are given regular holidays in bright light. They can also be given artificial light, but this should be from a special bulb or a fluorescent strip, as ordinary light bulbs generate too much heat.

LEFT Ferns and baskets seem to go together. Here the arching, wiry stems of maidenhair fern (*Adiantum capillus-veneris*) bend over the basket's edge and reach towards the handle. A begonia adds colour and highlights the fern's light foliage. Both plants like indirect light and moist air and compost, but the begonia will need more warmth in winter.

RIGHT Delta maidenhair fern (*Adiantum raddianum*) has a mass of delicate branching fronds with light-green foliage and some people find it easier to grow than other adiantums. The variety 'Fragrantissima' has dense and fragrant foliage.

TEMPERATURE

Temperature is just as important as light and growing medium, but this depends on the individual fern's place of origin and adaptability. As a general rule, most ferns dislike cold; ferns from temperate regions thrive at 10–15°C (50–59°F) – slightly cooler than most heated rooms – and those from the tropics and subtropics need an average 15.5–21°C (60–70°F). Most ferns like a winter rest at slightly lower temperatures, but few will survive at temperatures lower than 7°C (45°F), and for many ferns 10°C (50°F) is the minimum.

FEEDING

In summer, feed ferns every two to four weeks with weak liquid fertilizer. Do not mix to full strength as this can damage the delicate root systems. A few drops of fertilizer can be added occasionally to the water used for mist-spraying. Ferns should not be fed in winter if given a resting period.

REPOTTING

Repot ferns in spring, but only when their roots are filling the pot. Otherwise, simply scrape out and replace the top layer of the compost.

MISTING

Mist-spray as often as you like to keep the air around ferns moist, but never in low temperatures, at night, or when the plant is standing in bright sunlight.

RIGHT The height of the Hart's-tongue fern or Deer-tongue fern (*Phyllitis scolopendrium*), makes an excellent background for low-growing or trailing plants. The 'Cristatum', shown here, has particularly attractive fronds which are branched and crested.

A young *Blechnum gibbum* (often known as hard fern or rib fern) is kept moist by having its pot plunged into a peat-filled cache pot. This palm-like fern grows into a large specimen and develops a trunk as it ages.

Fishtail fern (*Cyrtomium falcatum*) and holly fern (*C. f.* 'Rochfordianum') are dependable ferns which are less susceptible to draughts and dry air than most. Standing the fern's pot in a saucer of wet pebbles provides adequate moisture.

EASY FERNS TO GROW
Asplenium bulbiferum
(mother fern, or **hen and chicken fern)** Related to bird's nest fern (*page 86*) and both are very undemanding. It produces new ferns rather like laying eggs – they grow from small brown bulbils on the fronds and drop off to grow in the soil below. Mature fronds are up to 90cm (3ft) long and 23cm (9in) wide. The plant likes medium light and average summer temperatures, with winter low of 10°C (50°F).

Cyrtomium falcatum **(holly fern)** An unusual plant, with glossy, leathery foliage, and has a height and spread of 50–60cm (20–24in). It grows well in low temperatures and dim light; give extra humidity to compensate if temperatures rise to around 21°C (70°) or more.

Davallia canariensis **(rabbit's foot** or **deer's foot fern)** One of the two hare's foot ferns. It has feathery foliage, and its sturdy, hairy rhizomes, which grow over the surface of the compost, form part of its attraction. Give medium light, and winter temperatures of 10–15.5°C (50–60°F).

Nephrolepis exaltata **(ladder** or **sword fern)** Similar to Boston fern (*see page 86*) and has a mass of fairly tough, tapering and semi-arching fronds 90cm (3ft) or more long. *N. e.* 'Whitmanii', the lace fern, has shorter fronds, 45cm (18in) long, with frilled edges. These ferns need bright, indirect light and average summer temperatures with winter temperatures of 13–16°C (55-61°F).

Pellaea rotundifolia **(button fern)** In complete contrast, this plant has 30cm (12in) fronds that are wiry stems with neat, button-shaped leaflets (pinnae) in deep green. It is 25–30cm (10–12in) high. It needs fairly bright, indirect light and normal summer temperatures with winter norms of 10–13°C (50–55°F).

ABOVE The hart's tongue fern (*Phyllitis scolopendrium*) has smooth, strap-like fronds with a marked central rib and wavy edges which, in the variety *P. s.* 'Crispum', are decoratively crimped and frilled. This, and their bright, clear, green colouring make a good contrast to smoother and darker foliage.

BELOW The button fern (*Pellaea rotundifolia*) is one of the smallest and prettiest of the ferns and goes well with a collection of small objects or with other small ferns and foliage plants. It is the perfect plant for a bedroom, as long as it can be kept away from draughts.

***Pteris cretica* varieties (brake or ribbon ferns)** The ribbony leaves of these plants have given them their name. *P. c.* 'Albolineata' is marked with white along the midribs and *P. c.* 'Alexandrae' has wavier fronds with crested tips. Young ferns are small and grow only slowly to about 23–38cm (9–15in) across and 30–45cm (12–18in) high. *Pteris tremula* is the brackeny, Australian trembling fern that eventually grows rather large, 60–90cm (2–3ft) high and almost as much across. All varieties need indirect light with some shade in summer, and also fairly low temperatures of 10–18°C (50–64°F) in the summer, which should not drop below around 7°C (45°F) during the winter months.

Ferns flourish when grown in a group, and smaller ferns can be planted together. Different species and varieties of the pteris ferns offer a range of light, dark and variegated foliage, broad and narrow, ribbony and feathered forms.

ABOVE A ribbon fern with variegated leaves (*Pteris cretica* 'Albo-lineata') stands in a white pot with nothing to detract from its slender, rippling fronds. The ribbon ferns need light shade in summer and flourish on a low table away from the window.

ABOVE A larger fern in a pot can leave a bare space below it when standing alone on a table. Here a trailing ivy and a bright blue pot fill the space and balance the arrangement. The fern is the tsusian holly fern (*Polystichum tsus-simense*), one of the shield ferns.

PROPAGATING FERNS

You can divide large ferns when repotting them, and some produce tiny plantlets that can be detached and potted up. You can also grow new ferns from the powdery spores produced in little capsules visible as rows of rusty-brown patches, usually on the undersides of the fronds. These grow into a green film of minuscule prothalli from which true ferns develop. The process can take several months, however.

Collect spores in a bag tied round a frond and grow them on moist, peaty compost in a seed tray or on a brick in a container of water. Pour boiling water over the compost to sterilize it and powder on the spores, using the tip of a knife. (Alternatively, lay a frond spore-side down on the surface.) Place the container in a polythene bag and keep it warm and semi-shaded until small plants develop from the green film that appears on the surface. Pot these up and give them more light and constant warmth.

GROWING AND DISPLAYING BROMELIADS

The typical houseplant bromeliad is a pineapple-like plant with a rosette of firm, fleshy leaves and, occasionally, an exotic, brightly coloured central flower. Some, similar in form, have an 'urn' or 'vase' at their centre, while a third group, the grey tillandsias or air plants, have less form and wander rootlessly. The bromeliads' roots are for anchoring it to supports such as the branches of trees rather than for feeding, and the plants flourish when grown in a pot that would be much too small for other plants of the same size. The tillandsias in particular are often grown without pots and can take their nourishment entirely from the surrounding air. All bromeliads are tropical or subtropical plants that make for very dramatic displays. In general they need high humidity and temperatures of 13–15.5°C (55–60°F), and up to 20°C (70°F) when actively growing in summer.

TILLANDSIAS

Tillandsias or air plants make an intriguing display anchored to shells or pebbles or pieces of driftwood. They have great curiosity value, but when neglected are a pitiful sight. Cryptanthus and fascicularia are ground-growing types also known as earth stars, and these too can be grown on stones, shells or bark.

2 Water the plants for the 'tree'. Remove the first plant from its pot and wrap the roots in sphagnum moss (*left*). Attach to the branch with plastic-coated wire.

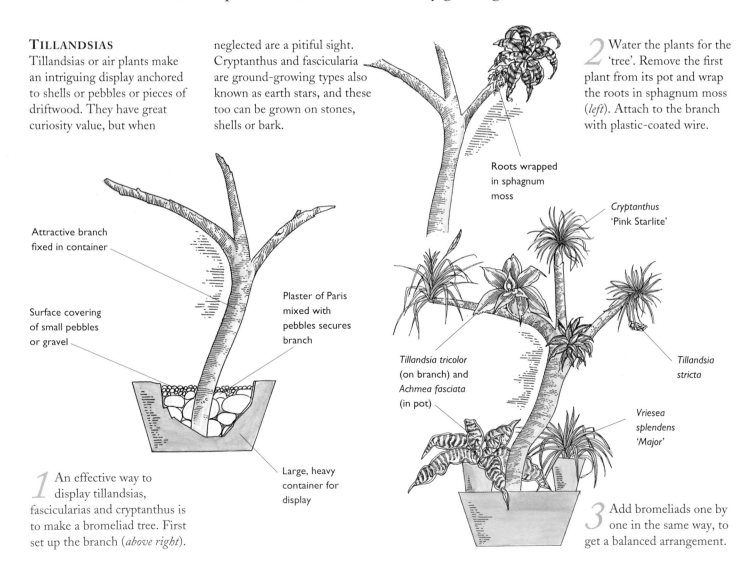

Attractive branch fixed in container

Surface covering of small pebbles or gravel

Plaster of Paris mixed with pebbles secures branch

Large, heavy container for display

Roots wrapped in sphagnum moss

Cryptanthus 'Pink Starlite'

Tillandsia stricta

Tillandsia tricolor (on branch) and *Achmea fasciata* (in pot)

Vriesea splendens 'Major'

1 An effective way to display tillandsias, fascicularias and cryptanthus is to make a bromeliad tree. First set up the branch (*above right*).

3 Add bromeliads one by one in the same way, to get a balanced arrangement.

AIR PLANTS

There are many small air plants for pot-free displays. Pot-bellied tillandsia (*Tillandsia circinnata*) has spiralling leaf-blades 20–45cm (8–18in) high; blushing bride (*T. ionantha*), 7.5–10cm (3–4in) high, has rosettes of silver-grey leaves which flush red before flowering; *T. geminiflora* has bracts of rosy-pink with tiny, violet flowers 15–20cm (6–8in) high; *T. ixioides* has a narrow, yellow flower head 13cm (5in) high.

BROMELIAD FEATURES
The bolder strap-leaved bromeliads such as ananas (pineapples), aechmeas (including urn plants) and vrieseas make striking plants grown in pots, and also adapt well to hanging baskets. There are also tillandsias (air plants) that grow well as specimens in pots and baskets. But many tillandsias and cryptanthus (earth stars) make interesting centrepieces attached to pieces of bark or driftwood or set in large shells and getting nourishment from the air as they do in their native forests. Cryptanthus are also well-suited to being grown in open-topped bottles and other glass containers.

The larger grey-leaved tillandsias are good plants for a hanging basket as they have arching foliage, are light, and need no watering.

An air plant attached to a piece of bleached and weathered driftwood makes a fascinating sight. The plants must be attached firmly and can be tied or even glued in place.

ABOVE A group of tillandsias, some planted in pebble-covered compost, others attached to bark, looks well in a plain pot. Air plants also seem to have an affinity with sea-shells. Simple surroundings and hard surfaces suit these plants best.

BROMELIADS FOR THE HOME

Most of the 'pineapple' and 'vase' or 'urn' bromeliads grow in the humid environment of the rain forests of Central and South America, dwelling in dappled light on the branches of trees. Bromeliads such as the fascicularia and cryptanthus, or earth stars, are generally ground dwellers that have adapted to the moist air of coastal areas or the inhospitable slopes of high mountain ranges.

Except for the tillandsias or air plants, most of which do not take to being grown in pots at all, bromeliads for the home should be grown in pots that are small for their size, in a very well-drained fibrous or peaty compost which is lime free, preferably with added charcoal. All bromeliads must have their needs for moisture met. All benefit from frequent mist-spraying with tepid, lime-free water, and this is essential for the tillandsias growing without pots. Bromeliads with central 'vases' or 'urns' should have these filled with fresh, soft, tepid water which is emptied and replaced from time to time, but the compost itself should be watered only moderately.

WARMTH AND FEEDING

Bromeliads need warm air (*see page 92 for details*). A test of this is that the water in the centre of 'vase' and 'urn' types should evaporate away – if not it will become stagnant. In the wild they get their nourishment from organic debris in the air and, in the case of 'vase' and 'urn' types, falling into their centres. In the home they should be watered with a balanced fertilizer diluted to half-strength every six to eight weeks. This can also occasionally be added to the water with which they are sprayed and, except for blushing bromeliad (*Nidularium fulgens*), to the water in their central reservoirs. Like most flowering plants bromeliads need to be watered more when flower buds appear and during active growth. To maintain a good level of humidity you can stand the plants on trays of wet pebbles – which can be look attractive – or use a mist spray.

FLOWERING

The main attraction of bromeliads is their leaves and forms, but many also bear beautiful flower spikes, generally consisting of colourful bracts and small and insignificant flowers. Be prepared to wait, as flower spikes normally appear only on mature plants. After flowering the plant may die, but not before it has produced offsets which can be potted up to make new plants. Most bromeliads grown in pots have a rosette of leaves and a central reservoir.

The common pineapple (*Ananas comosus*) was first introduced and cultivated for its fruit, but is now grown as an ornamental plant. Its leaves take on a reddish tint when it is kept in good light, and in the variety 'Variegatus' they are bordered in cream.

AECHMEAS

Aechmeas have a pronounced central reservoir, and these are the plants known as 'vase' or 'urn' plants. The offsets that grow round the parent plant should be detached when they are about 15cm (6in) high and grown on in very small pots.

***Aechmea fasciata* (urn plant or silver vase)** This plant has strong, broad, curving leaves of a dull, bluish-green, marked all over with powdery silver-white. The mature plant has leaves up to 50cm (20in) long and 6cm (2½in) wide and bears a flower head of pink bracts and tiny, blue flowers. The flower can last for several months but the plant begins to die after flowering.

As long as the air is kept moist the plant will enjoy temperatures of up to 26°C (79°F) in summer. It should be kept cooler in winter but not below 15°C (60°F).

Earth stars (*Cryptanthus*) have wavy-edged leaves — either well-coloured or with contrasting bands of colour. Coming from Brazil, they love warmth and humidity, and most of those grown as houseplants are not more than 7.5–13cm (3–5in) high, making them good plants for growing in glass containers.

***Aechmea chantinii* (Amazonian zebra plant)** This aechmea also has beautifully marked leaves, banded in grey and spine-edged. Its flower head is red and spiky.

***Aechmea fulgens* (coral berry)** The common name of this plant is derived from the red berries that follow on from the blue flowers. It has very dark-green spine-edged leaves and in the variety *A. f.* 'Discolor' the undersides of the leaves are purple.

RIGHT The bold architectural form and pale-blue bloom of the leaves of the urn plant (*Aechmea fasciata*) make it a striking plant even before it flowers. It can stand out against other foliage plants or make a fine, single specimen.

ABOVE In contrast to *Aechmea fasciata*, *Aechmea spectabilis* has a delicate, spiky flower head.

Tillandsia flabellata is one of the green-leaved tillandsias that are normally grown in a pot. Its leaves are long and tapering, and can take on a reddish tint. In late summer and autumn it produces flower heads of colourful red bracts.

RIGHT Pineapples (*Ananas*) eventually bear colourful flowers but are principally grown for their striking spine-edged leaves. Ivory pineapple (*A. comosus* 'Variegatus') has the benefits of compact form and attractive ivory coloured striping.

VRIESEAS

Vrieseas have deeply cupped rosettes of strappy leaves and many are grown for the attractive leaves alone. These varieties include *Vriesea hieroglyphica*, king of the bromeliads, which has purple-marked, yellowish-green leaves that can be up to 60cm (2ft) long and 10cm (4in) wide, and *V. fenestralis*, which has yellowish-green leaves that are speckled with dark green on the upperside and a reddish-purple on the underside.

Vriesea splendens or flaming sword produces a succession of long-lasting flower heads of bright-red overlapping bracts on stems 60cm (2ft) high from a rosette of dark-green, banded leaves about 40cm (16in) long. The rosette, which forms a central 'cup', dies very slowly when the flowering has finished. It needs a temperature of up to 27°C (80°F), with high humidity.

PINEAPPLE PLANTS

Although they do produce flowers the ananas or pineapple plants are grown chiefly for their foliage. The two forms most grown are *Ananas comosus* 'Variegatus', the ivory pineapple, and *A. bracteatus* 'Striatus', the red pineapple. Both have tall, stiff leaves with sharply serrated edges that arch as they get to full length of some 60cm (2ft). Ivory pineapple has ivory-coloured stripes and red pineapple has cream and deep-pink stripes.

BELOW King of the bromeliads (*Vriesea hieroglyphica*) forms a rosette of yellow-green leaves irregularly patterned with dark purple. It flowers in spring, bearing yellow, tubular heads.

EARTH STARS

All the bromeliads described so far are large, 'stand alone' plants. The earth stars or cryptanthus are small in comparison. There are many earth stars and all are grown for their striped or banded foliage, arranged in the typical rosette and often with wavy or saw-toothed edges. They produce numerous offsets, and the best way to detach these to form new plants is to remove the parent plant from its pot first and pull off the offsets before replanting the parent. Earth stars need normal summer temperatures and a steady 15.5°C (60°F) in winter. They thrive in glass containers.

Cryptanthus bivittatus is the most popular species. Its leaves have wavy, serrated edges and are 10–15cm (4–6in) long, striped green and pinkish-yellow. *C. b.* 'Tricolor' is larger and has stripes of olive-green, white and pink. *C. fosterianus* or pheasant leaf has gingery-brown leaves brindled in grey and remarkably like the tail feathers of a pheasant and *C. zonatus* is known as the zebra earth star because of its beautifully banded leaves.

TILLANDSIAS

The tillandsia species which grow well in pots have long, grassy, rather untidy looking leaves and spectacular flat fish- or quill-shaped flowers made up of overlapping bracts. Many of these are delightful, fairly small plants between 23cm (8in) and 45cm (18in) high. Pink quill, *T. cyanea*, for example, with its vivid-pink flower head, is 23cm (9in) high. All tillandsias prefer very high summer temperatures of up to 27°C (80°F) and 10–15°C (50–59°F) in winter although they are tough plants and can survive at temperatures as low as 5°C (41°F) as long as the compost is kept only just slightly moist.

OTHER BROMELIADS

The other main groups of bromeliads are the billbergias, the guzmanias, the neoregelias and the nidulariums.

Billbergias are especially easy bromeliads to grow. They produce spectacular flower heads on long, arching stems from the centres of the rosettes, and although each rosette dies after it has flowered, the plant has several at once, in different stages of development. Two popular billbergias are *B. nutans* and *B.* × 'Windii.

The most popular guzmania is *G. lingulata* or scarlet star. It has fairly narrow green leaves up to 50cm (20in) long and eventually produces a flower head consisting of flaring red bracts. This is another relatively easy bromeliad

which tolerates a range of normal room temperatures as long as it has plenty of humidity. It should not be fed but its funnel should always have fresh, soft water.

The most popular neoregelia is *N. carolinae* 'Tricolor', one of two plants often called blushing bromeliad. Its leaves are very glossy and painted in cream and pink stripes. The whole plant blushes red from the centre before it flowers and retains this colouring for several months. The low flower head appears at the centre of the rosette. The species *N. spectabilis* has red-tipped green leaves which become purple-brown at the centre.

Nidulariums are also known as blushing bromeliads. The variety *N. innocentii*, however, is individually known as bird's nest bromeliad. At its centre is a rosette of very short leaves which blush before it flowers (the bird's nest) and this is surrounded by longer broad green leaves.

ABOVE *Guzmania lingulata* 'Minor' has the rosette of broad, strap-like leaves typical of many bromeliads. Leaf colour and the red or yellow bracts of the flower heads are intensified when the plant is grown in bright light. The plant is sometimes known as orange star or scarlet star.

The blushing bromeliad, *Neoregelia carolinae*, has bright-green leaves which blush purple and red at the plant's centre before flowering. In the variety 'Tricolor' (below) the leaves are attractively striped in cream; the whole plant flushes deep pink as it flowers and keeps this colouring for several months.

ABOVE *Neoregelia carolinae* 'Flandria' has particularly broad leaves, generously edged and narrowly striped in cream. Not yet widely available, it is well worth looking out for.

CACTI AND SUCCULENTS

People become addicted to cacti and they are certainly very collectable plants and ideal for a sunny windowsill. We associate cacti with the desert, and indeed many of them grow in the desert regions of Central and South America. But other cacti come from as far north as Canada, and many are native to rainforests. Like the bromeliads, many cacti are epiphytes, and the forest-dwelling species grow over the forest trees. The desert-dwelling cacti can survive long periods without rainfall, getting their moisture from dew or mist, and storing nutrients and moisture in their tissues. This is a defining characteristic of succulent plants and it is this capacity that defines cacti as succulents.

Botanically, what makes a cactus a cactus is that it has growths known as areoles, which are cushioned growing points that are technically compressed lateral branches. Spines, 'wool', flowers and offsets all grow from the areoles. Many succulents resemble cacti in almost every way – even to growing spines – but not in this distinguishing feature. In all but one genus of cactus (*Pereskia*), the plants do not have leaves, but spines or scales.

CACTI

Having no leaves, the cacti store nutrients and water in the body of the plant, which consists, botanically, of a stem. The 'bodies' of cacti are generally globular or cylindrical in shape, although the opuntia cacti have round, segmented stems that are flattened out and the epiphyllums have stems that look more like strap-shaped leaves which are again segmented. Many cacti have prominent spines, barbs or bristles, and some have woolly hair, and every cactus in fact has spines even though these may be small and seemingly insignificant. It is not always known or appreciated that all cacti are actually flowering plants that will flower regularly if well looked after.

ABOVE Like most of the notocacti, *Notocactus grossei* is neat and spherical. It is easy to care for and produces delicate yellow flowers at the top of its round stem. Its long, reddish-brown spines are part of its charm.
OPPOSITE An imaginatively arranged group of cacti makes an absorbing display. Here barrel, columnar and 'lollipop' shapes intermix with two opuntias, which are recognized by their flattened pads.

SUCCULENTS

Succulent means, literally, juicy, and succulent plants have leaves or stems that are swollen with juices. These are the stored water and nutrients that enable the plants to survive in harsh conditions all over the world. They normally have a glossy or leathery appearance and their texture helps to protect them from excessive moisture loss.

There is a huge range of succulent plants that can be grown in the home and some of them are among the very easiest plants to care for, making them ideal for beginners, for children and for people who have to be away from home a lot. But, as with all plants, you have to understand their nature to grow them successfully.

GROWING AND DISPLAYING

From the breathtakingly beautiful, such as the orchid or pond lily cactus (*Epiphyllum* 'Ackermanii') and other large-flowered epiphyllums, to the frankly weird and wonderful, such as sea urchin cactus (*Astrophytum asterias*) or the hairy old man cactus (*Cephalocereus senilis*), cacti and succulents make a fine display and it is a shame that they are not more widely cultivated. The reason for this probably stems from their undemanding natures – for these plants will survive almost any treatment except complete over-indulgence. This has resulted in cacti and succulents that are neglected and left to gather dust on people's windowsills at one extreme and plants that are rotting from overwatering at the other. They need very bright light, fresh air, and a cool, dry winter rest.

While the forest cacti tend to have a trailing habit and large flowers, making them perfect for individual display in hanging baskets, the interesting shapes and textures of the desert types, and of many succulent plants, can be highlighted by a grouped display where they can be compared and contrasted. A group of small cacti or succulents planted together in one bowl is particularly effective, although larger specimens such as some aloes and agaves (succulents) look best in a pot of their own, as can the more curious plants such as sun cactus (*Heleocereus speciosus*).

CACTUS GARDENS

Any large, shallow dish can be used as a container for a cactus garden. Select desert cacti and small succulents for this and the plants will then share similar growing and care requirements. Since these plants all need maximum light, you need to select a container that is the right shape and size to fit in the lightest place that you can offer.

Arrange the plants fairly closely to avoid the 'spotted dick' or 'dot' effect – this is an effect caused by groups of plants that have been arranged with little form or structure – and choose a variety of shapes and sizes. A layer of fine grit spread over the compost provides an attractive and suitably dry surface for the cacti, and clean pebbles arranged between the plants completes the effect.

A mixed group of small cacti is perfect for a broad, sunny windowsill. Patience is required for the first three or four years and then many cacti will burst into bloom.

FOREST CACTI

The forest cacti are very different from the dry-land plants. They usually have spectacularly beautiful hanging flowers growing from the tips of segmented stems that look like chains of fleshy leaves and they grow in a trailing manner because of their habit of growing over trees. Through this habit they are used to dappled shade, although, being tropical and subtropical plants, they need quite bright light; so they should be kept in good light but protected from strong sun. Like all rainforest plants they need light, lime-free, well-drained compost and high humidity, and should be frequently mist-sprayed with tepid soft water. They should be rested in a cool place at a temperature of 10–13°C (50–55°F) after flowering and watered sparingly until flower buds appear; then water them moderately and feed weekly with a fairly weak solution of balanced fertilizer as well as moving to a spot with higher temperatures.

CARING FOR DESERT CACTI

For desert cacti the compost must be very well drained. Special cactus compost, or any potting compost with added sharp sand or gravel, can be used. They should be well watered with tepid water in spring and summer but the compost should be allowed to become almost completely dry between waterings; in winter they should be kept almost completely dry, especially in cool conditions.

Cacti should be fed about every three weeks when in active growth with well-diluted tomato plant fertilizer.

Most cacti do best in winter temperatures of 10–13°C (50–55°F) but can withstand temperatures as low as 5°C (41°F). Repot only when the roots absolutely fill the pot.

BELOW LEFT The epiphyllums are forest cacti – rainforest plants which, in summer, produce some of the most beautiful of all flowers. They cross-breed very readily and many hybrids have now been bred to be grown as houseplants, including 'Reward'. Epiphyllum flowers are usually about 10–15cm (4–6in) wide. They are often given the common name of orchid cactus.

In contrast to the flowering cacti there are those that are grown for their unusual forms and textures. These include several hairy species, such as *Espostoa melanostele*. When young this is a globe-shaped plant but it develops into a tall and columnar specimen as it ages.

PLANTS IN POTS

Cacti can also look very charming arranged simply in a row, all potted in similar or completely matching pots. Cacti such as oriental moon cactus (*Gymnocalycium mihanovichii* 'Friedrichii'), which come with differently coloured heads and are otherwise alike, look at their best displayed in this simple but attractive way.

Most cacti and succulents need the maximum light possible, and are therefore suitable for the sunniest of windowsills. This light-loving characteristic can be exploited to the full by fixing shelves across a sunny window and standing rows of neatly potted cacti on them. You could also arrange the pots in a low-sided basket or a wicker tray. Make sure that the plants are turned frequently so that all parts get equal exposure to the full light.

CHOOSING CACTI

There is an almost bewildering range of cacti to grow at home and every garden centre has a fairly wide selection. Some cacti (for example, the forest-growing Christmas and Easter types, properly called *Schlumbergera × buckleyi* and *Rhipsalidopsis gaertneri* respectively but, confusingly, often known as zygocactus and schlumbergera) are sold as seasonal gift plants in department stores, too. It is best to buy cacti that are in flower, as they can take several years to reach maturity and flowering age. Check them over carefully, making sure they are sound with no trace of rot or areas that are dry or shrivelled. They should be just the right size for their pot – not too small but not showing signs of roots being cramped. Make sure that they are not exposed to sudden draughts of cold air on their way home. Once you get a taste for cacti you will find that you need to go to a specialist nursery for the more unusual specimens.

EASY DESERT CACTI

The following cacti are easily grown and brought into flower.

***Astrophytum myriostigma* (bishop's cap cactus)** This cactus has ribbed sides which are gathered up in the shape of a bishop's mitre. It is smooth and greyish-green, speckled with white and its ribs are marked with white, felty blobs (areoles). When about four or five years old it produces a succession of scented, lemon-yellow flowers in summer. Astrophytums are known collectively as star cacti, and there are six other species all of similar shape and with decorative spines or woolly spots. All reach a maximum height of about 15cm (6in) and can be grown from seed.

Borzicactus aureiflora Often sold under its old name of *Matucana*, this cactus has a slightly flattened globe shape, and bright yellow flowers sprout from the top of the stem in summer. Bright light, and fairly generous watering and fortnightly feeding in summer encourage flowering.

Barrel cactus (*Echinocactus grusonii*) has golden-yellow spines and a deeply ribbed stem. It is a favourite choice for a non-flowering cactus. The slow-growing globe is topped with a crown of yellow hairs, while the spines on the ribs are aggressively sharp.

Bishop's cap cactus (*Astrophytum myriostigma*) is a cushiony, spineless cactus with from four to eight ribs. It grows best (like all the astrophytums) in a very light, sunny position and when fed once every two weeks in summer with a tomato fertilizer. The species is covered with silvery scales, but the variety 'Nudem' (shown here) has smooth, dark green skin.

***Chamaecereus sylvestrii*
(peanut cactus** or **gherkin
cactus)** The common name of
this cactus is derived from its
rows of rather marrow-shaped
stems which look like bristle-
covered gherkins or peanut
pods. It is fast growing and it
produces its red or deep-orange
flowers in late spring. Several
hybrids are available but these
are less fast growing. It needs
to be brought out of its winter
resting period in early spring.

Dolichothele longimamma is
a small and long-lived cactus
with narrow, fleshy projections,
each with a lightly spined tip.
During the summer it
produces shiny, bright-yellow,
upright, bell-shaped flowers
with many petals.

Mammillarias include the
most popular of all cacti – and
there are literally hundreds of
species. They form cushions,
mounds – some cylindrical –
and 'cauliflower' heads, all
covered in numerous tiny
spines. In spring all bear either
a few large flowers or several
smaller ones, which are
followed by fruits. But beware
– many mammillarias also have
vicious hooks.

Notocactus (ball cacti) This
species of cacti are mostly
small, taking ten years to reach
up to 18cm (7in). They are
spherical and spiny, some
becoming cylindrical as they
age. Flowers, which can be
disproportionately large, are
produced on the top of the
'ball'. *N. ottonis* is a typical
small ball cactus which has a
mass of yellow flowers in
spring. *N. leninghausii* or
golden ball cactus grows up to
60cm (2ft), and is liked for its
golden spines. Ball cacti are
easily grown from seed.

LEFT Peanut cactus (*Chamaecereus
sylvestrii*) has short stems like a fistful
of bright green gherkins. In the
species the flowers are bright, deep
red and are produced in abundance
throughout the spring and summer.

LEFT Mammillarias are
among the best of the
cacti for beginners to
grow. They are often
densely covered with
downy or spiky spines,
and are generally
globular. They tend to
remain small, and to
produce neat little
coronets of brightly
coloured flowers, as in
Mammillaria hahniana.

Goat's horn cactus
(*Astrophytum capricorne*) has
dark, untidy, curled spines
and becomes more columnar
as it ages. It produces yellow
flowers in summer. The species
Astrophytum myriostigma (see
page 102) is covered in
silvery-white scales.

Rebutias (crown cactus)
These small cacti are perhaps
the easiest to grow. Their
common name describes their
flowers which often form a
ring around the base of the
plant. They have funnelled,
many-petalled flowers and
form mounds 10–15cm (4–6in)
high. *R. miniscula* comes in
forms with red or violet
flowers; *R. aureiflora* is studded
with yellow flowers; *R. senilis*
has flowers in red, yellow or
lilac. Rebutias may die quite
soon after flowering, but they
produce offsets from which
new plants can be grown.

CACTI GROWN FOR THEIR SHAPES OR SPINES

Some cacti have to be very large and mature before they flower and these are among the cacti that are grown for their curious shapes or for their unusual spines. A good selection would include some of the following:

***Cephalocereus senilis* (old man cactus)** Has a columnar stem completely covered by an 'old man's beard' of white hairs. In the wild it lives to a great age, and can grow to 12m (40ft) high. Eventually, at home, the beards need washing with detergent, in the fresh air on a warm, dry day.

***Cereus peruvianus* (Peruvian cereus)** Another tall cactus which can grow to 90cm (3ft) fairly quickly in a warm, sunny room. Its columns are blue-green, ribbed and spined. *C. p.* 'Monstrosus' is an interesting form of this species of cactus with gargoyle-like side branches.

***Cleistocactus* (closed cacti)** Tall, slender stems with their narrow ribs ornamented by neat spines and woolly areoles. One or two forms are branched or trailing. A popular variety is *C. strausii* or silver torch which has silvery-white spines and which grows to about 1.2m (4ft) indoors.

The intriguing hibotan cactus plants (*Gymnocalycium mihanovichii* 'Friedrichii') are produced by grafting brightly coloured heads on to green stems.

ABOVE TOP Most of the notocacti are round and attractively ribbed and spined, *Notocactus claviceps* has golden spines and quickly forms clusters of large and small spheres, topped with patches of prominent white areoles.

ABOVE *Rebutia miniscula* 'Grandiflora' produces long, deep-red flowers, which spring up from close to the base of the stem, while it is still only about 5cm (2in) in diameter. Otherwise similar varieties flower in orange and pink.

Echinocactus grusonii (**golden barrel**) A little spherical cactus which grows incredibly slowly, developing regularly spaced ribs studded with starry golden spines. The top of the 'barrel' is slightly depressed and covered with golden wool.

Ferocactus (**barrel cacti**) Also of spherical shape and can slowly reach 60cm (2ft) or more in height. They have ferocious, stiff, often barbed spines. The species *F. latispinus* is bright green, with neater, pinkish-yellow spines, and only slowly grows beyond 10cm (4in) in diameter.

Opuntia (**prickly pears**) Most of the opuntias are the multiple-lollipop type, with flattened stems growing in rounded segments. Among those popular as houseplants are *O. brasiliensis*, which makes a large plant; *O. microdasys*, bunny ears, true to its name in shape and covered in round golden-tufted pads, and *O. rufida* or red bunny ears, which has brownish-red tufts, both growing to about 30cm (1ft) high.

O. subulata (**awl cactus**), is unusual in having cylindrical, many-branched stems covered in projecting awl-shaped, green leaves and yellowish-spined areoles. Although this plant grows to 3m (10ft) in the wild it is seldom taller than 75cm (30in) in the home.

LEFT *Epiphyllum* 'Ackermanii' and related hybrids generally have deep-red and scarlet flowers. They flower very prolifically, especially if kept in the same pot for several years.

ABOVE Many ferocacti are grown mainly for their fierce curling spines, but *F. echidne* has short erect spines on its barrel-shaped stem and is crowned with flowers.

TRAILING CACTI

Aporocactus flagelliformis (rat's tail cactus) – long, thin, trailing stems covered with large cerise flowers in spring* (treat as desert); *Epiphyllum cooperi* hybrids (orchid cactus) – huge, fragrant, white or yellow flowers open at night*; *Heliocereus speciosus* (sun cactus) – firm, spiny, green, trailing stems; *Rhipsalis cassutha* (mistletoe cactus) – berry-bearing, angular, branching stems*; *Schlumbergera truncata* hybrids (claw cactus) – similar to Christmas and Easter cactus with winter flowers in gorgeous colours*; Willcoxia – thin, winding, grey-green stems with small white spines or down. Plants marked * are forest types, see page 101.

SUCCULENTS

Apart from the cacti, there are some fifty or more families of plants that can be classified as succulents. The cacti are in origin confined almost exclusively to the Americas, but the rest of the succulents come also from Africa and parts of Europe. Like the desert cacti they are dry-land plants (many of them grow side by side with cacti) and they nearly all have the same needs for plentiful sun, a well-draining compost, watering freely in summer, but only when the compost has become nearly dry, and scant watering in winter, when they should be kept at temperatures around 10°C (50°F). In summer, most succulents need a well-diluted fertilizer feed about every three weeks, and fresh air rather than humidity. Some succulents store water and nutrients in their swollen, fleshy leaves (the leaf succulents), others, the stem succulents, have tough, fleshy stems, and a third kind, the root succulents, have swollen roots of various kinds in which their reserves are stored.

ALOES, AGAVES AND HAWORTHIAS

Aloes are plants with rosettes of stiff, leathery, tooth-edged leaves, broad at the base and tapering to a point. Their leaves are often blotched, striped, banded or striated. Flowers are bell-shaped – generally orange – and grow in cones on tall, erect stems. There are small aloes, such as *A. humilis*, the hedgehog aloe, with bluish, white-toothed leaves 10cm (4in) high and *A. aristata*, the brush or lace aloe, which has white-spotted leaves and grows some 10–15cm (4–6in) high. Medium-sized ones include 30cm (12in) high *A. variegata*, the partridge-breasted aloe with its white-patterned leaves, and one of the giants is *A. arborescens*, the tree aloe, which can easily grow to 90cm (3ft) in a container.

Agaves are very similar to aloes though their 'teeth' tend to be more widely spaced, and both teeth and leaf stripes tend to be bolder. *A. victoriae-reginae* is perhaps the favourite as a houseplant; its many dark-

green, spine-tipped leaves are neatly edged with white and it is only 15cm (6in) high.

Haworthias have strong, rather plump, broad tapering leaves, which grow from small stems in packed rosettes and are often said to be 'warty'. In *H. margaritifera*, the pearl plant, the rosette is so dense as to be ball-like, and the leaves are encrusted with decorative pearly 'warts'.

BELOW The many euphorbias have no one distinctive form. The remarkable gingham golf ball (*Euphorbia obesa*) (left) is dome-shaped, but other euphorbias have branching, tree-like stems, some have tall, slim columnar stems and some are spiny and irregularly shaped. Gasterias have firm and fleshy, tapering leaves that form flattened or untidy rosettes. Ox tongue (*Gasteria verrucosa*) (centre) has neatly paired leaves which are covered in tiny warts.

The century plant *Agave americana* 'Marginata' (right) has the characteristic broad, wavy leaves, which in this variety are edged and narrowly striped with creamy-yellow.

RIGHT Succulents of contrasting appearance are seen in zebra haworthia (*Haworthia fasciata*) (left) and candle plant (*Kleinia articulata*) (right). Haworthias come from Africa, where they grow partly in the shade of large plants; although they need dry, warm air, they are not at their best in bright sun, which affects their colouring. Their preference for some shade and their small size make them easily accommodated houseplants. Kleinias have tall stems up to 60cm (2ft) high, and in the candle plant these have a blue bloom and produce yellow flowers in summer.

CRASSULAS AND SEDUMS

There are many crassulas, generally with smaller, rounded or sometimes triangular leaves and succulent, sometimes twisting stems. Jade plant or money tree (*C. argentea*) is a well-known houseplant. It looks like a tiny and exotic tree with a sturdy, fleshy stem and equally fleshy deep-green, waxy leaves. The cactus-like rat tail plant (*C. lycopodioides*) shows how different plants of the same genus can be. It has upright branching stems in light green, completely covered in little triangular, fleshy leaves from top to bottom.

Sedums are equally fleshy and some have cylindrical 'jelly bean' leaves. Many have branching, prostrate stems. In donkey's tail or burro's tail (*S. morganianum*) the stems can trail to 90cm (3ft) in a hanging basket, sometimes bearing pink flowers at the ends throughout the summer. These stems are crowded with bright-green leaves, while in the similar *S. sieboldii* 'Medio-variegatum' the leaves are a pink-patterned, cool blue-grey.

BELOW *Aloe aristata* has orange-pink flowers on tall stems which spring from dense rosettes of sharply pointed, white-edged leaves. The rosette is only 10–15cm (4–6in) high, with the flower stems 90cm (12in) high.

OTHER SUCCULENT HOUSEPLANTS

Cotyledon undulata (silver crown) – leaves like fleshy cabbage leaves, also with blue bloom; *Echeveria derenbergii* (painted lady) – rosettes of piled-up fleshy leaves with blue bloom, and orange flowers on towering stems; *Euphorbia obesa* (gingham golf ball/Turkish temple) – cactus-like pincushion with grey and yellow 'gingham' marking and crimped ridging; *Faucaria tigrine* (tiger jaws) – friendly little soft-teethed tiger mouths opening round deep-yellow summer flowers; *Lithops* species (living stones) – small, fleshy, flat-topped leaves just like little desert stones; daisy-like flowers spring up in the crevices; *Pachyphytum oviferum* (moonstones/sugar almond plant) leaves with a mauve bloom like grapes or little eggs; *Sedum pachyphyllum* (jelly bean plant) – mound of jelly beans; *Senecio rowleyianus* (string of beads) – creeping or trailing stems strung with pretty, bluish 'beads' of succulent globular leaves.

GLOSSARY OF HOUSEPLANT TERMS

Acaricide A chemical used to kill parasitic spider mites, such as red spider mites.

Acid Compost or soil with a pH below 7.0. Most plants grow best in slightly acid conditions, about pH 6.5.

Adventitious roots Roots that develop from unusual positions, such as on leaves and stems.

Aerial roots These are roots that appear from a stem and above soil level, as with the Swiss cheese plant (*Monstera deliciosa*), some ivies and orchids. Their prime task is to gain support for stems.

Air layering A method of propagating plants by encouraging roots to form on stems. The rubber plant (*Ficus elastica*) is often increased in this way.

Alkaline Compost or soil with a pH above 7.0.

Alternate Buds or leaves that grow on opposite sides of a stem or shoot.

Annual A plant that completes its life-cycle within a year; seeds germinate, the plant grows, and flowers and seeds are produced within one growing season.

Anther Part of a stamen, the male reproductive part of a flower. A stamen is formed of a stalk (filament), with an anther at its top. Pollen grains form within an anther.

Aphids Perhaps the main pest of house and garden plants and also known as greenfly. They breed rapidly in spring and summer, clustering around the soft parts of flowers, shoots, stems and leaves. They suck sap, causing debilitation as well as spreading viruses.

Apical The tip of a shoot or branch.

Areole A modified sideshoot, resembling a tiny hump, unique to cacti. It bears spines, hairs, bristles or wool.

Aroid A plant belonging to the Arum Family and including anthuriums, dieffenbachias, monsteras and philodendrons.

Asexual A non-sexual way to increase plants, such as by cuttings, layering and division rather than seed.

Axil The junction between a leaf and stem, from where sideshoots or flowers may develop.

Bigeneric hybrid A plant produced by crossing two plants from different genera. This is indicated by a cross positioned in front of the plant's name. For instance, the ivy tree (× *Fatshedera lizei*) is a cross between a form of the false castor oil plant (*Fatsia japonica* 'Moseri' and also known as the Japanese fatsia), and the Irish ivy (*Hedera helix* 'Hibernica').

Bleeding The loss of sap from a cut stem. Rubber plants (ficus) exude sap when stems are severed.

Blind A plant whose growing point has not developed properly.

Bloom This has two meanings, either flowers or a powdery coating on flowers, stems or leaves.

Bottle gardening Growing plants in environments created by carboys and other large glass jars. Sometimes the container is stoppered and the air inside recycled by plants, while others are left open.

Bract A modified leaf; some provide protection for a flower, while others assume the role of petals and are the main attraction. Poinsettia (*Euphorbia pulcherrima*) has brightly coloured bracts.

Bromeliad A member of the Bromeliaceae family. Many have rosettes of leaves that form urns. A few of them are epiphytes.

Bulb A storage organ with a bud-like structure. It is formed of fleshy scales attached at their base to a flattened stem called the basal plate.

Bulbil An immature and miniature bulb that usually grows at the base of another bulb. However, some plants, such as the mother fern (*Asplenium bulbiferum*), develop plantlets on their leaves which are also known as bulbils. These can be detached carefully using tweezers and encouraged to form roots.

Cactus A succulent plant belonging to the Cactaceae family. All cacti are characterized by having areoles.

Calcicole A plant that likes lime in its compost.

Calcifuge A plant that dislikes lime in its compost.

Calyx The sepals as a whole and forming the outer ring of a flower.

Capillary action The passage of water upwards through potting compost or soil. The finer the soil particles, the higher the rise of moisture. The same principle is used in self-watering systems for plants in pots in sun rooms, conservatories and greenhouses.

Carboy A large, somewhat round or pear-shaped glass bottle used as a container for plants.

Clone A plant raised vegetatively from another plant, so ensuring that it is identical in every particular to the parent.

Columnar A plant that rises vertically, usually

used to refer to trees and conifers but also to describe some cacti.

Compost Has two meanings. The first refers to the medium in which plants grow when in pots or other containers, and in North America is known as potting compost. It is formed of a mixture of loam, sharp sand and peat, plus fertilizers, or peat and fertilizers. The second meaning is material produced after the total decay of vegetable waste when placed on a compost heap in a garden. It is either dug into soil or spread over the surface as a mulch.

Corolla The ring of petals in a flower that create the main display.

Corona Petals in certain plants that form a cup or trumpet, as in daffodils.

Cristate Crested, used to describe some ferns and cacti, as well as a few forms of houseplants. For example, cockscomb (*Celosia argentea cristata*) creates crested flower heads.

Crock A piece of broken clay pot put in the base of a clay pot to prevent compost blocking the drainage hole.

Cultivar A variety raised in cultivation by selective breeding.

Cutting A vegetative method of propagating plants by

which a severed piece of a plant is encouraged to develop roots.

Damping down Increasing the humidity in a sun room, conservatory or greenhouse by using a fine-rose watering-can to spray water on the floor and around plants. It is best carried out early in the day so that excess moisture dries before nightfall.

Dead-heading The removal of faded and dead flowers to encourage the development of further flowers. It also helps to prevent diseases infecting decaying flowers.

Dibber A rounded, blunt-pointed tool for making planting holes in compost and soil outdoors.

Division A vegetative method of propagation, involving dividing the stems and roots of plants.

Dormancy The resting period of a plant or seed.

Double flowers Flowers with more than the normal number of petals.

Drawn Thin and spindly shoots or plants, after having been grown in crowded or dark conditions.

Epiphyte A plant that grows above ground level, attached to trees, rocks and, sometimes, other plants. Epiphytes do not take nourishment from their host, but just use it for support. Many orchids and bromeliads are epiphytes.

Etiolated Blanched and spindly, the result of being grown in poor light.

F1 The first filial generation and the result of a cross between two pure-bred and unrelated parents. F1 hybrids are large, strong and uniform, but their seeds will

not produce replicas of the parents.

Fern A perennial, flowerless plant that produces spores.

Fertilization The sexual union of male (pollen) and female (ovule) parts.

Filament The slender stalk that supports the anthers of a flower. Collectively, the anthers and filaments are the stamen.

Fimbriate Fringed and usually referring to a flower or petal.

Flore-pleno Refers to flowers that have a larger than normal number of petals.

Floret A small flower that, with others, forms a flower head, such as in chrysanthemums and other members of the Compositae family.

Frond Leaf of a palm or fern.

Fungicide A chemical used to eradicate or deter fungal diseases.

Germination The process that occurs within a seed when given moisture, air and warmth. The seed's coat ruptures and a seed leaf (or seed leaves) grows towards the light, while a root grows downwards. However, to most gardeners germination is when shoots appear through the surface of potting compost or soil.

Glaucous Greyish-green or bluish-green and usually

applied to describe stems, leaves or fruits.

Glochid A small, hooked hair growing on some cacti.

Half-hardy A plant that can withstand fairly low temperatures but needs protection from frost.

Half-hardy annual An annual which is raised in gentle warmth in late winter or early spring. Some of them are grown as houseplants.

Hermaphrodite Having both male and female organs in the same flower.

Hormone A growth-regulating chemical that occurs naturally in both plant and animal tissue. Synthetic hormones are widely used to encourage cuttings to develop roots.

Hydroponics The growing of plants without the aid of soil. It is also known as hydroculture.

Inflorescence Part of a plant that bears flowers.

Insectivorous A plant that is adapted to trap, kill and digest insects such as small flies. In this way it is able to supplement food that its environment is not able to provide.

Internodal The part of a stem or shoot between two leaf-joints (nodes).

Joint The junction of a shoot and stem, or a leaf and a leaf-stalk. These are also known as nodes.

Juvenile leaf Several houseplants have, when young, differently shaped leaves from those on mature plants. For example, when young the false aralia (*Dizygotheca elegantissima*) has long, wavy-edged leaves. In mature specimens, these broaden and lose their delicate, lacy appearance.

Layering A vegetative way to increase plants, involving lowering stems and slightly burying them in soil or compost. By creating a kink, twist, bend or slit in the part of the stem that is buried, the flow of sap is restricted and roots are encouraged to develop.

Leaflet Some leaves are formed of several small leaves, each known as a leaflet. A leaflet is characterized by not having a bud in its axil.

Leggy Plants that become tall and spindly, often through being kept in dark places.

Mist propagation A mechanical device that sprays leaves with fine water droplets. This keeps cuttings cool, as well as reducing their need for moisture before they develop roots.

Neutral Compost that is neither acid nor alkaline and with a pH of 7.0. Horticultural neutral is considered to be between 6.5 and 7.0.

Node A leaf-joint or position where a shoot grows from a stem or branch.

Peat Partly decomposed vegetable material, usually with an acid nature. Because of its capacity to retain water it is used in seed and potting composts.

Perennial Usually used when referring to herbaceous perennials, but also applied to any plant that lives for several years, such as trees and shrubs.

Petiole A leaf-stalk.

Photosynthesis The food-building process when chlorophyll in leaves is activated by sunlight and, together with moisture absorbed by roots and carbon dioxide absorbed through stoma from the atmosphere, creates growth.

pH A logarithmic scale used to define the acidity or alkalinity of a soil-water solution. The scale ranges from 0 to 14: neutral is 7.0, with figures above indicating increasing alkalinity and, below, increasing acidity.

Pinching out Removing the tip of a shoot to encourage the development of sideshoots.

Pip Two distinct meanings – the seed of some fruits, such as apples and pears, and the rootstock of plants such as lily-of-the-valley (*Convallaria majalis*).

Plantlet An offset produced on a plant's leaves or stem.

Pot-bound When a plant fills its pot with roots and requires to be repotted.

Potting-on Transferring an established plant from one pot to another.

Potting-up Transferring a young plant from a seed tray into a pot.

Pricking off Transferring seedlings from the seed tray in which they were sown into other seed trays and given wider spacing.

Propagation The raising of new plants.

Pseudobulb The thickened stem of some orchids.

Root-ball The packed ball of roots and compost in which a houseplant grows.

Root hair The fine, feeding roots that develop on roots to absorb nutrients.

Seed leaf The first leaf (sometimes two) that appear after germination.

Seedling A young plant produced after a seed germinates.

Self-coloured Flowers with just one colour, in contrast to bicoloured (two colours) and multicoloured (several shades).

Sessile Leaves and flowers that do not have a stalk or stem attaching them to the plant.

Softwood cutting A cutting formed of a non-woody shoot.

Spadix A dense spike of tiny flowers, usually enclosed in a spathe.

Spathe A large bract or pair or bracts, often brightly coloured, surrounding a spadix.

Spores The reproductive cells of non-flowering plants.

Stamen The male part of a flower.

Stigma The female part of a flower.

Stipule Leaf-like sheaths at the base of some flower stalks.

Stoma Minute holes – usually in the underside of a leaf – that enable an exchange of gases between the plant and the surrounding air (*see Photosynthesis*).

Stop The removal of a growing tip to encourage the development of sideshoots.

Stove plant A plant that requires an environment with a high temperature.

Strain Seed-raised plants from a common ancestor.

Strike The rooting of a cutting.

Style Part of the female reproductive element of a flower, linking the stigma to the ovary.

Succulent Any plant with thick and fleshy leaves. Cacti are succulent plants, but not all succulents are cacti.

Systemic Chemicals that enter a plant's tissue, killing sucking and biting insects.

Tendril A thread-like growth that enables some climbers to cling to their supports.

Terrarium A glass container, partly or wholly enclosed, used to house plants.

Terrestrial Plants that grow in soil at ground level.

Top dressing Replacing the surface soil of plants in large containers with fresh potting compost. Plants are normally top-dressed because they are too large to be repotted into a larger pot.

Turgid Plants that are firm and full of moisture.

Variegated Multicoloured leaves.

Variety A natural occurring variation within a species. The term is also commonly used to include both true varieties and variations which have occurred through human endeavours, correctly termed cultivars.

Vegetative propagation Methods of increasing plants, including the division of roots, layering, grafting, air-layering, budding and taking cuttings.

INDEX